THINGS BOGANS LIKE

how to recognise the twenty-first century bogan

E. CHAS MCSWEEN, ENRON HUBBARD, FLASH JOHNSON,
HUNTER MCKENZIE-SMYTHE, INTRAVENUS DE MILO
AND MICHAEL JAYFOX

T0363309

hachette
AUSTRALIA

All internal photographs courtesy as follows: Page 2, *Bogan Place*, Newspix/Adam Ward; p. 4 *Melbourne Cup Day*, Newspix/Andrew Tauber; p. 20 *Roulette at Star City*, Newspix/Cameron Richardson; p. 34 *Max Markson*, Newspix/Patrick Hamilton; p. 47 *Brynne Gordon on Logie red carpet*, Newspix/Julie Kiriacoudis; p. 52 *Leaning Tower of Pisa*, istockphoto.com; p. 68 *André Rieu on Neighbours*, Newspix/David Caird; p. 84 *Boxing Day sales*, Newspix/Fiona Hamilton; p. 104 *Krispy Kreme opening at Fountain Gate*, Newspix/Craig Hughes; p. 116 *Pizza street*, Newspix/Pip Blackwood; p. 118 *Pills*, istockphoto.com; p. 21 *Bodybuilders*, istockphoto.com; p. 134 *Charles and Diana wedding*, Newspix; p. 152 *Man on elephant*, Bigstockphoto.com; p. 158 *Cronulla riot*, Newspix/Noel Kessel; p. 170 *Big Day Out*, (top) Newspix/Bruce Magilton, (bottom) Newspix/Jeff Camden; p. 182 *Andrew Bolt*, Newspix/Shaney Balcombe; p.198 *Army*, Newspix/Troy Rodgers; p. 206 *King Kyle*, Newspix/Stephen Cooper; p. 210 *Tara Reid at Ed Hardy store*, Newspix/Justin Lloyd; p. 222 *Man in dress*, Newspix/Megan Brayley; p.234 *Schapelle Corby with sister's front cover edition of Ralph*, Newspix/Lukman S Bintaro; p. 241 *Facebook ban*, Newspix/Stuart Milligan; p. 248 *Buddha statue*, istockphoto.com; p. 258 *Light heavyweight bout*, Newspix/Brett Costello; 268 *Road rage*, Newspix/Nicki Connolly.

hachette
AUSTRALIA

First published in Australia and New Zealand in 2010
by Hachette Australia
(an imprint of Hachette Australia Pty Limited)
Level 17, 207 Kent Street, Sydney NSW 2000
www.hachette.com.au

This edition published in 2013

Copyright © E. Chas McSween, Enron Hubbard, Flash Johnson, Hunter McKenzie-Smythe, Intravenus De Milo, Michael JayFox 2010, 2013

National Library of Australia
Cataloguing-in-Publication data:

Things bogans like / E. Chas McSween ... [et al.]

978 0 7336 3041 5 (pbk.)

Personality and culture.
Australian wit and humour.
Australia – Social life and customs – Humour.

Other Authors / Contributors: McSween, E. Chas. Hubbard, Enron. Johnson, Flash. McKenzie-Smythe, Hunter. De Milo, Intravenus. JayFox, Michael.

305.50994

Front cover photographs courtesy of Shutterstock
Cover photo of André Rieu and Richard Wilkins courtesy of Newspix/Julie Kiriacoudis
Typeset by Shaun Jury
Author photographs courtesy of Ed Butler and Matt Hollingsworth
Cover design by Design by Committee/Blue Cork
Internal design and cover adaption by Christabella Designs
Printed in Australia by McPherson's Printing Group

MIX
Paper from
responsible sources
FSC® C001695
www.fsc.org

The paper this book is printed on is certified against the Forest Stewardship Council® Standards. McPherson's Printing Group holds FSC® chain of custody certification SA-COC-005379. FSC® promotes environmentally responsible, socially beneficial and economically viable management of the world's forests.

C**o**ntents

Bis

You will find them in a laneway bar with no signage on the door. They will be sipping beers with no English on the labels. They will be talking amongst themselves about things that are too avant-garde to appear in a textbook. They are the authors of *Things Bogans Like*. Six gentlemen, brought together by their desire to define and catalogue the modern bogan for the benefit of our nation. These are their stories.

Intravenus De Milo

Born in Wien in 1983 to an Indian mother and Luxembourgian father, Intravenus De Milo spent much of his childhood wanting to learn the reasons for things. After travelling through Africa and the Middle East, Intravenus completed his first degree in the arts from Trinity College, Dublin at the age of nineteen. Not satisfied with the myopic lens of subjectivity through which he saw the world, Intravenus moved to the prestigious Maxx Planck Institute for High Energy Physics to explore the origin and composition of dark matter.

Then, bored with far too acute an understanding of the universe, Intravenus decided to move as far away from intellectualism and scholarship as possible. This took him to Australia where the author has spent the last few years, smug in the satisfaction that he is pretty much the smartest person in the country. Intravenus is unmarried, has no children and wants all hot tubs to be cold. In his spare time, Intravenus likes to win Olympic medals in badminton.

Hunter McKenzie-Smythe

Born to the twin pastoral fortunes of the McKenzies and the Smythes, Hunter spent the greater part of his childhood and adolescence in expensive boarding schools. On holidays, Hunter would read great sections of the comprehensively unread libraries in his family's various townhouses, abandoned as he was by his parents, twirling around the world having affairs with interesting yet profoundly empty people.

After completing an arts degree majoring in cultural studies and art history, Hunter skied the world, routinely rejected his father's requests to manage the family's various business interests, and bedded as many beautiful men and women as time permitted. This continued until, while recovering from a peyote-fuelled ski-doo accident, Hunter experienced an epiphany and converted to Sunni

Islam. His appetite for knowledge replenished, Hunter became fluent in Arabic and Farsi, studied Islamic law and international relations, and now shares his time between Melbourne and his apartment in Sana'a, Yemen.

Flash Johnson

Born from an egg on a Peruvian mountaintop in 1986, Flash spent his early years studying the rise and fall of ancient South American civilisations. It quickly became obvious to Flash that the decline of every once-great ancient empire had been caused by large groups of late arrivers who brought with them overconsumption, violence, garish fashion, racism and attention-seeking behaviour. These serial civilisation destroyers were dubbed, collectively, the 'bogan'.

Having solved the mysteries of the past, and acutely aware of the imminent threat that the modern bogan poses to today's global community, Flash turned his attention to preventing another bogan-induced catastrophe of the ages. His studies took him to the University of Manchester, where he simultaneously completed an arts degree and studied the bogan-repellent properties of local bands such as The Smiths and Joy Division.

Now ready to tackle the epicentre of the bogan's assault on society, Flash set sail for Australia – the site of the world's most advanced bogan colony; an island facing epidemic levels of bogan per capita. He resides in Melbourne to this day, and travels only via city laneways. In his spare time he is a semi-professional Uno player. He is unmarried, and wants all highways to be low.

Enron Hubbard

Ron was born in a hospital in Eltham, in Melbourne's north-east. He grew up in Eltham, and attended primary and secondary schools in Eltham. Having endured an interminable commute to study his arts degree outside of Eltham, he now resides in Eltham, sharing his time between there and Meadowbank, the Sydney equivalent of Eltham.

Such prolonged exposure to regions of high bogan quotient would ordinarily be fatal to most. However, like kids born in Chernobyl with seven heads, Ron developed an immunity to fluorescence and stupidity after stapling a flannel shirt to his chest.

Since his arrest for civil unrest while defending battery hens in Tamworth, New South Wales, militant vegan Ron has reinvented himself as a hermit, fearful of reprisals from angry bogans who value their low-cost, high-quantity egg and poultry goods.

E. Chas McSween

Born in Malawi in 1981, E. Chas was orphaned into the care of Masai warriors in Tanzania, learning the arts of tracking, hunting and shamanism. He also developed the superhuman endurance for which the Masai are renowned, which proved incredibly useful when, at the age of eight, he was adopted by visiting celebrity bogan Greg Evans and relocated to a household full of Ken Done prints and Jive Bunny CDs.

Growing up in the bogan hub of Glen Waverley, in Melbourne's south-east, E. Chas rapidly developed a deep, intuitive under-standing of the bogan, its motivations and behaviours. After taking seven years to complete his arts degree, he relocated to Padova to study art history, where he developed his twin passions of 17th century European architecture and 18th century European architecture.

E. Chas now rents an apartment in Melbourne's inner north (he does not intend to buy) with his defacto partner (he does not intend to marry) and his Great Dane, Heidegger (he does not intend to have children), compiling his soon-to-be bestselling biography of Johann Bernhard Fischer von Erlach. In between professional abseiling tournaments and drinking cafe lattes, E. Chas dedicates his remaining time to ghost writing articles for creationist former AFL footballers.

Michael Jayfox

Born in Melbourne in the summer of Bob Hawke's first prime ministerial campaign, Michael Jayfox spent some of his youth observing the bogan in the lush habitat of Victoria's Latrobe Valley while his parents managed a government department designed to restrict the bogan's treacherous ways. Jayfox later undertook an arts degree at a private institution in Johannesburg, where he also developed passions for ornithology and archaeology. He then returned to Melbourne for postgraduate study in marketing and economics.

Initially planning to sell the bogan maxtreme products that it didn't need, he became distracted by the study of the bogan creature itself. Struck by the bogan's fascinating blend of pride, ignorance, hypocrisy and impulsiveness, he began writing of its ways. In 2004, Jayfox was informed by a salesman that a famous actor had appropriated his name. In the future, Jayfox hopes to become the first person to jump over a shark on water skis while reciting Chaucer.

F●reword:

What is a bogan today?

An excellent question. The word bogan has had a bad rap of late. Intended as an insult, it historically focused on Kingswoods, VB or (gasp!) MB, wife-beater singlets, utes, mullets, and names like Sharon and Barry. But what's wrong with these things? At the end of the day, bogan was a word that wealthy or middle-class people could toss around as a means of insulting poor people without actually saying that they didn't want poor people around. That's unfair. These days gentlemen called Baz sinking a tin of VB in a flannel shirt are more likely to be (a) a hipster in the inner suburbs or (b) a really top bloke.

This bogan is harmless. He does not colonise. He does not post racist rants on news website blogs. He does not buy enough tickets to ensure P!nk plays 75 straight nights at Rod Laver Arena. No, he is happy to pick up tickets to the occasional AC/DC tour, and beyond that he stays home, nursing a cold drink, watching telly. He is happy. He does not invade every bar that is mentioned in the paper's entertainment section, hoping to spot a minor celebrity. He does not attend classy restaurants wearing paint-stained jeans and painfully selfconscious Converse. He doesn't go to a gig by a buzz band, then proceed to get spastic drunk and participate in screaming contests three metres from the stage.

The adoption of bogan as an insult means that the word needs a better definition. The old use of the word conceals the new, modern bogan. The bogan with money. The bogan with aspirations. The bogan with Ed Hardy t-shirts. And this is no mere Australian phenomenon – every country has their own bogan. While there are national variations, the crux of our discussion remains the same.

The bogan today defies income strata, class, race, creed, gender, religion and logic. The bogan is defined by what it does, what it says and, most importantly, what it buys. Those who choose to deny the bogan on the basis of its North Shore home, their stockbroking career or their massive trust fund choose not to see the bogan. They merely see old class battles revisited. Likewise, the bogan is no mere 'tradie'. Indeed, the modern bogan romanticises and fantasises about tradies. Even if some tradies remain low-income workers, many bogans are affluent. And they set themselves apart by conforming as furiously, and conspicuously, as possible.

We will endeavour to highlight the new bogan lifestyle. And we will fight against it. Welcome to *Things Bogans Like*. This book does not kill fascists.

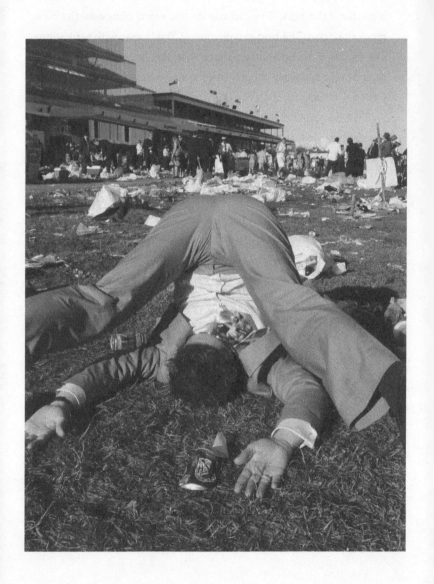

ASPIRATIONAL BOGANS

Misspelling their kids' names

Like much of the western world, the bogan is on a constant quest for self-actualisation. However, its quest to be unique tends to revolve around a level of cultural conformity that borders on the criminal. And nowhere is this more obvious than when they bless their offspring with their names.

Naming a child is a permanent thing, or should be, and the bogan parent takes care to ensure that its own pursuit of awesome individualism is reflected in its young. There is no better way to achieve this, thinks the new parent, than to give the baby a 'unique' name. This, unfortunately for the poor offspring, is where the process falls down. Rather than actually bestowing their newborn with a genuinely one-of-a-kind name – or at least an uncommon one – the bogan merely takes a common one, then misspells it. Bogans love remixes of songs, the maxtreme version of something familiar, changed just enough that the bogan can tell itself that it's listening to a cool new song. This love of the remix is manifested when they get the chance to name a child. Ever met a Hayleigh? A Breeyanah? A Jorja? A Kayleb? Probably many, but you may have thought they were Hayley, Brianna, Georgia or Caleb. *These* kids will be spelling out their names to all and sundry for the next 80 years. Because they're a unique snowflake, each and every one.

How about a Jaxon? Or a Jacksen? Or even a Jakxsen? A recent, and related, trend in bogan names is to simply replace a first name with a surname. Then misspell it. But it doesn't end there – the aspirational bogan has also identified the opportunity to finally own some luxury goods. By calling their children Chanel or Armani. The bogan believes that conferring such a name on its child will ensure future prosperity for both child and parent, and as a result feels no obligation to put effort into properly raising the child once it is born.

Of course, the end result of all this creativity is that instead of five Adams in a class attempting to distinguish themselves from each other, there are now Riley, Reilly, Rhylee, Rhylie, Rylee, Ryley and Rylie getting into stoushes over whose dad has the biggest flat screen/best surround sound system. The bogan parent has thus consigned its remixed child to being a B-side on the vinyl of life.

The Melbourne Cup

Taken from National Geographic . . .

Once a year, the ~~Black Grouse~~ South Victorian crested bogan congregates in the ~~Azore Islands~~ general admission area of Flemington, off ~~Portugal's coast~~ Epsom Road, for their annual rut. Many of these creatures travel ~~several thousand kilometres~~ for about an hour to arrive in mid-spring, for this is the only time of year that the entire ~~Black Grouse~~ bogan population is in the one place, at the one time.

The ~~Black Grouse~~ bogans are extremely energetic ~~birds~~ and they display constantly. Each male has his own area into which he tries to entice a female. They emit a turkey-like noise which reaches a crescendo when, periodically, they all display at the same time. They regularly challenge their neighbours, with a different call which sounds like ~~an avian~~ a bogan approximation of 'come on then'. Many fights ensue. Some of this is done for effect when a female passes by, but some is serious and quite vicious.

There are also sites where the females tend to congregate, and space near these display areas is fiercely contested. After a number of mock charges one male will attempt to escalate from mere display, with the sole intention of establishing dominance over his opponents. Almost every male has a ~~bare patch on the back of~~ stupid hat on his head, while some retain the ~~plumage~~ ruffled, directionless hair of their youth. Those that do have this spend a great deal of time grooming it, particularly early in the day.

Most also have a ~~red patch on their breast~~ pair of white leather shoes that contrast sharply with the black of their ~~feathers~~ suit, and is thought to be a secondary means of display. The weaker ~~birds~~ bogans who spend their time on the outer edge of the display area have often had all their ~~tail feathers~~ money removed. They look a sorry sight compared to their ~~elegant~~ peers.

The bogan has taken to the Melbourne Cup like an aspiring actress to a terminally ill oil magnate. The combination of comfortable, familiar surrounds, ample (low quality) booze and a chance to uncover as much female skin under the guise of 'formal attire' as possible has made the lure of racing's biggest day impossible to resist. In 2009, the Cup was a far cry from the genteel, debonair event of yesteryear. Today, as dusk descends over the looming trash pile that Flemington has become in a matter of hours, female bogans can be seen vomiting daintily, stilettos in hand, while a male bogan hovers optimistically nearby . . .

Malapropisms

At some point on the journey from childhood to adulthood, the social power balance shifts. Among 14-year-olds, the superior social animal is the physical specimen: the best looking girl, the top athlete, the guy who manages to combine the boyish good looks of a young Brad Pitt with the unrestrained violence of Mike Tyson.

Those whom they lord it over are the nerds. Those who, bereft of the genetic assistance their socially superior peers are blessed with, are forced to adapt to survive. They get smart.

Years later, and the power balance has begun to shift. The physical specimens, lacking the need to cultivate an awareness of life, culture or basic grammar, have found themselves at a disadvantage in the adult world where brains have suddenly and unexpectedly become paramount. That many of these former jocks and glamours have evolved into today's bogans is unsurprising. Their response to this social shift, however, is not. They fake it. By inserting words that sound similar to something they once overheard on the ABC into ordinary sentences, they believe that they can enhance their social standing. With hilarious results.

The bogan malapropism has evolved into many variants. First is the effective mispronunciation of a mundane, and ostensibly appropriate, word. Common among these are the two classics 'for all intensive purposes' and 'please be pacific'. However, these are easily remedied, and display at least a grasp of vocabulary, if not spelling.

One of the classic examples, not strictly a malapropism, is certainly the most common. It is, literally, the misuse of the word 'literally'. As in 'It was so hot yesterday, I was literally on fire' or 'I literally died crossing the road this morning'. Another is stunning in its linguistic faux-profundity. It is the use of words that sound impressive, in the hope of slotting unobtrusively into a sentence. Often incorrect, sometimes they are actually complete antonyms of the intended meaning. If the bogan feels the need to point out that it is eating at a 'classy' restaurant, it can be safely assumed that the restaurant is, in fact, Nandos.

When the bogan unintentionally malapropises, it will often rapidly search for escapegoat. It will assure its friends that it knows what's going on, and compliment them on their receptiveness. It will then inform everyone it knows about its maxtreme exacerbation with constantly being misunderestimated. Irregardless, it will plough on, mangling the language with a Herculean persistence, until one day, its regiment of misappropriate words simply runs dry, and it miscontinues its efforts.

Self-help books

The bogan will tell you it likes to read. Having the means to attend university and briefly flirt with academic theories of psychology and fulfilment, it will also loudly claim that it aspires to self-actualisation, a state of being everything it could ever hope to be.

Stubbornly impeding the progress towards this lofty goal is the fact that bogans *love* shortcuts. Be it get-rich-quick schemes, examining a limited number of habits of 'highly effective' individuals, or simply seeking an effortless strategy to living superbly, the bogan cannot wait for the next quick fix to a better life. However, lacking the patience and introspective ability to actually better itself, the bogan hungrily seeks out the next bestseller that shamelessly adorns the gift shop in the Tiger Airways terminal.

Proudly bearing claims such as '*The ultimate guide to spiritual enlightenment in seven days*' or '*A practical guide to personal and financial freedom*', the bogan, it would seem, simply cannot resist the allure of potentially getting rich and achieving inner peace for a paltry $29.95 (in heady moments of either enthusiasm or guilt). This makes the bogan a prime culprit for the burgeoning self-help publishing industry and intellectual cretins/life coaches/gurus who model themselves on Anthony Robbins.

Ostensibly rooted in psychological theory, the 'self-help' pandemic has infected a staggering number of unsuspecting and gullible bogans nationwide. Bearing an uncanny resemblance to low quality home-spun advice, the bogan is tricked into thinking it is helping itself, while blindly digesting a stranger's manipulative swill neatly condensed into 50 pages. Filled with pearls of wisdom such as *'If you can't, you must, if you must, you can'* and *'If you do what you've always done, you'll get what you've always gotten'*, it is little wonder that the helplessly malleable bogan mind takes to this drivel like a pensioner to a poker machine.

While the bogan is unlikely to read more than 10% of the self-improvement products it purchases, the mere presence of these brightly coloured, excitedly titled tomes on the IKEA bookshelf (next to the *Twilight* series and Thailand Lonely Planet guide) are designed to impress visitors. It secretly believes any wisdom contained within will be transferred to all occupants of the room like one of those air fresheners it plugs into a power point.

It is sadly only a matter of time until titles such as *Get Confident, Stupid* or *Kidneys for Sale: How to Maximise Your Body's Potential* become the next big thing.

McMansions

Bogan visionary John Landy was one of the first to tap into its brain stem and recognise the bogan's need for sheer size. When he had the Big Banana built next to his fruit stall in1964, bogans gravitated to it like single mothers to a stockbroker's Christmas party. Soon, it wasn't enough for the bogan to just visit big things; it wanted to live in one.

A couple of decades ago, the McMansion arrived, an answer to bogan prayers. It wasn't better than the houses that came before it, but good heavens it was bigger. The average size of new homes in Australia has gone on to grow by 40.3% between 1985 and 2003, as the bogan became aware that it 'deserved' a formal living area, a rumpus room, a parents' retreat, an en suite, a study, a formal lounge, and a large void near the stairs that allowed it to view different parts of its McMansion without moving its feet. A home that, at first glance, looked reminiscent of a celebrity home.

Of course, the ballooning size of the bogan's domestic ambitions meant that such dwellings could not really be situated on small blocks. Unwilling to make any compromises in this respect, the avalanche of poorly serviced cut-price housing estates continued across the outskirts of cities nationwide. These estate names uniformly contain misleading words such as springs, meadows, gardens and park. Bogan families in these estates become entirely reliant on cars for transport, and bleat angrily when the petrol price is not to their liking. They do not pause to consider that the price is high partly because bogan families are using so much of it, a direct consequence of their housing decisions.

Pesky laws about how close a dwelling can be to the edge of the block of land threatened to derail the bogan's desire for maxtremely proportioned housing. Bogan-friendly builders solved this by constructing a neo-Georgian cube with no eaves, allowing the house to loom over the fence like a 43-square-metre peeping tom. The bogan's noble battle against the extremes of the Australian climate is then won by the constant use of heaters and air conditioners to overcome the atrocious inefficiency of the architecture. Upon receipt of its massive energy bill, the bogan will complain that the power companies are ripping it off.

In order to put ridiculously huge houses within reach of the financially impulsive bogan, builders take phenomenal amounts of shortcuts on the shoddily fitted out McMansion. Once the flashy silver oven breaks and the paper-thin feature wall cracks, it becomes clear that the housing estate is ten years away from being a generic and unserviced bogan ghetto. It's the great Australian dream come true.

Delta Goodrem

Delta Goodrem, lusty songbird that she is, had built a bogan empire by the time she was twenty. The combination of bogan-standard good looks, vanilla bland balladry and the perception of purity were deeply appealing to the female bogan's need to idolise the Diana, and the male bogan's desire to violate it, all to the soundtrack of a mid-nineties sub-Whitney Houston piano number. When Goodrem tragically contracted non-Hodgkin's lymphoma in 2003, the selectively compassionate bogan was able to forge a deep spiritual connection with this chanteuse it had never met, extending its deepest sympathies and allowing it to feel that it had contributed directly to Goodrem's fortunate recovery.

Then, sometime after releasing her third album, Goodrem decided that this singing caper was for schmucks. She came to the realisation that so many before her had come to – that bogan bucks can be made far more easily than by actually doing stuff. She decided to lend her renewed flowing locks and glamour looks to selling shampoo. And decided she liked it.

The bogan likes buying things. Delta likes selling things. In some cosmic alignment only seen every 5000 years or in the occasional Schwarzenegger film, Goodrem began to mine a vein of bogan bucks so rich as to boggle the mind of amateurs like publicist Max Markson. Markson must constantly be alert to the proclivities of the bogan – which celebrities it is interested in reading/ talking about – then manipulate the bogan media in order to increase his payments to the maxtreme. Delta, by contrast, rocks up at a photo studio, poses for some shots, records a sound bite or two, then walks back to her mansion and watches the bogan bucks roll in.

What's more, she has successfully targeted her product promotions to hit on some incredibly potent bogan pressure points. She sells ProActiv skin care, with a formula so advanced that the bogan could not possibly understand it, and thus believes that it is entirely responsible for Delta's alabaster skin. She advertises Sunsilk shampoo, which the bogan naturally insists is the reason for her cascading reams of golden blonde hair. She advertises So Good soy milk, to ensure the bogan can revel in her ability to sell hippy milk to hippies. She sells the music magazine in News Ltd's Thursday papers, the same magazine that routinely informs the bogan about how outstanding the latest Australian Idol's album is, via a series of hard-hitting interviews.

Most importantly though, she sells Wii Sports and Nintendo DS Brain Training. These two products are so face-meltingly bogan that their combination with such a bogan witch doctor is the proverbial bogan bug-zapper. Wii Sports advertises to the bogan that it can lose weight and get fit by standing still and watching television. Brain Training advertises that it can make the bogan smarter by pointing a stylus at an array of third-grade problem-solving challenges on a portable screen.

Now fatter, dumber, with greasy hair, equally greasy skin, a love of Lady Gaga and an inexplicable addiction to soy milk – its long-held soy allergy notwithstanding – the bogan waits with bated breath to see how on earth Delta can make its life better next.

Louis Vuitton, Moët et Hennessy

Years ago, marketeers figured out that correctly branding a product allowed a company to charge four trillion times as much, and that bogans would still purchase it. Some companies were better at pulling this off than others, with the concept of European prestige appearing to resonate particularly well inside the cavernous chamber of the bogan skull. This was despite the bogan's only experience of Europe being a 12-day vomit-packed blur aboard a Contiki bus.

In the late 1980s, the scattered configuration of European luxury companies began to clot into magnetic lumps of bogan joy. Moët et Chandon, Hennessy and Louis Vuitton were brought under the one roof, and more and more additions were made after then. The French parent company believed it had uncovered the ultimate formula for savaging bogan bank accounts, and they wanted to do it with as many brands as possible.

Indeed, the bogan is willing to send itself deep into the pit of insolvency in order to acquire LVMH goods. Female bogans display 100% interest in Louis Vuitton products, and are willing to pay 20% interest to Mastercard in order to bolster their egos in this manner. The male bogan is not immune either, as it is prone to spending $3000 on a TAG Heuer watch, another LVMH brand. TAG Heuer understands the bogan's warped concept of mateship, evidenced by the brand conspicuously sticking with its multimillion-dollar sponsorship of disgraced-then-forgiven sport star and adulterous womaniser Tiger Woods. This increases the bogan's desire to purchase the watch.

Even though the bogan rarely drinks champagne and has no idea of the difference between a subtle, effervescent drop and $5 sparkling sauvignon, it will celebrate occasions by conspicuously swilling a $70 bottle of Moët. It does this out of its deep compulsion to live like a celebrity, and it will retain the empty bottle in a prominent position in its house for many months. The bogan will loudly describe the experience to anyone who will listen. It is not interested in other brands, unless someone has told it that its favourite celebrity drinks Veuve Clicquot. However, the bogan is even worse at pronouncing that brand name, meaning it will generally stick with either its Mowee or Mowert.

LVMH has spun numerous other sticky webs to trap any airborne bogan bucks. Brands such as Marc Jacobs, DKNY, Fendi and Kenzo have been known to penetrate the bogan's oversized Christian Dior sunglasses . . . the parent brand of the entire LVMH empire. This galaxy of glittering brands has sent thousands of bogans broke. At this point, they will run from the tax department by jumping on a Jetstar flight to Bali or Thailand, where they will purchase five different knockoff Louis Vuitton handbags, three pairs of Dior sunglasses, and a duty free bottle of Moët.

The Lynx effect

Today's classy woman makes informed decisions about the partner she chooses. She wants a man who knows at what temperature to properly serve cheese. A man who knows how to correctly decant cellared red wine to remove sediment. A man with at least a passing knowledge of American modernist literature. A man who's not going to run off with the first slapper who rubs up against him on the dance floor, just as the Vengabus' arrival appears imminent.

In short, the bogan male needs help to pick up a classy chick. Thankfully, help has arrived in the form of the Lynx effect – an effect caused by scent so primally potent, females of the species instantly devolve to making mating decisions based purely on pheromonal response. After all, it's named after a wild, toothsome big cat. One spray of this magic concoction, and even the most terminally ugly and crass bogan male can mack with the most ferociously unattainable corporate lawyer-cum-lingerie model.

The Lynx effect is so powerful, in fact, that other male grooming companies sent their super-awesome scientists off on missions to incorporate it into their slightly-less-masculine products. What emerged was a collection of hideously fragrant armpit saturators so powerful that it's a wonder that bogans everywhere aren't busy forming harems of slavering, fecund concubines. And the Lynx effect spread to other deodorants. Brut, once the realm of older men looking for some generic, affordable suave chic, became 'STILL BRUTALLY MALE', making said middle-aged men the supposed target for the very slappers their wives are supposedly terrified of.

The smells created are so new to humankind, the companies eventually abandoned trying to give them properly adjectival names, and instead assigned them words like 'Accelerate', 'Sharp Focus', 'Pulse', 'Vice' and 'Dimension'. Of course, with smells so powerful, and names so powerful, it stood to reason that the cans' propellant be capable of generating individual ozone holes in three sprays. Thus, the bogan can empty a can once a week, soon enough to maintain a rotating roster of nostril-assaulting musk.

On Thursday, the bogan's 'Java' day, it exits its home to head off for work, a vaporous cloud wafting gently behind it, looking for all the world like heat haze. It wanders into the office, all winks and finger-guns, before slapping its co-worker on the rump and asking 'Toots' how she's doing. On Friday he can no longer afford access to the Lynx effect.

Franchises

It's not that the bogan is afraid. The bogan is maxtreme, and not afraid of anything. It's more that . . . well, the independent bakery might have rats on the floor, and who knows what the charcoal chicken store is putting in its gravy? It's not fear, it's . . . it's standards. Yeah, standards. The bogan has standards. Standards that can only be met when the front of the shop has a familiar logo that the bogan has seen in other suburbs and towns too. It's best for the bogan to be nourished by the Colonel's mystery gravy instead.

Despite Jim Penman holding a PhD in the bogan-derided intellectual field of history, he has managed to become the bearded cartoon that pacifies many areas of the bogan's life. Starting with a mowing business in 1982, the bogan now trusts Jim to clean its carpets, install its antennas, even to wash its dog. His ever-expanding universe of franchised service businesses mean that the bogan may never need to invite an unbranded human into its McMansion again.

Franchised brands do so much more than just make the bogan feel calm in its confusing world, they are also crucial *papier-mâché* for its thin latex identity. When the bogan wants others to perceive it as healthy, it will circle the foodcourt clasping a Boost Juice, logo facing outwards. When the bogan wants to seem sophisticated, into Gloria Jean's cosmopolitan maw it shall march. And after a big afternoon at Endota Spa, what better look for the bogan female than to collect its nascent ADHD charlatans from a 14-hour stint at the local ABC Learning Centre. While ABC is in administration due to bad debts and maxtremely shonky accounting practices, the bogan is less afraid of franchised corporate crooks than the potential paedophiles working at community child care centres.

From time to time, the enterprising bogan will express a desire to buy its own franchise of a brand that it enjoys purchasing from. While there is a 95% chance that this will never become anything more than talk, most of the other 5% will involve the bogan overpaying for a poorly conceived or located business, and quickly learning that being an owner-operator is much harder work than earning penalty rates to join moronic Facebook groups on someone else's time. At this point the bogan will exit the business at a loss, and tell its friends that it is 'exploring other opportunities'.

The bogan's overwhelming urge to remain well inside its own narrow comfort zone has driven Australia to become the most densely franchised nation on earth. So set in its ways does the bogan become that it is unwilling to even dabble in unfamiliar franchises, despite their inherent franchised trustworthiness. That said, the bogan's resistance to change is swiftly broken down once a celebrity endorsement or other marketing campaign is undertaken. For while each bogan is a unique snowflake, franchises allow them to be as precisely as unique as each other.

B●GANOMICS

Residential property investment

The bogan hates being told what to do, hates having its movements restricted, and hates feeling obliged to anyone. This is an important reason why it loves purchasing investment properties: so it can tell someone what to do, restrict their movements and have someone feel obliged to them.

While the bogan finds other classes of investment to be annoyingly abstract, residential property provides the bogan with the ability to cut corners on maintenance, and to smugly survey its empire. Worried about tales told to it by uninformed bogan friends about stock market losses, it will enthusiastically lap up advice dispensed by the same uninformed bogan friends about the magic of negative gearing on residential property. Indeed, it is likely that the bogan followed its herd and invested in a Telstra stock offering, only to be infuriated by years of poor performance. The impatient bogan then sells low and decries the entire stock market as 'dodgy'.

With this hatred of dodginess fresh in its mind, the bogan will seek refuge in the fantastic 25% returns promised at property seminars conducted by fine businessmen such as Henry Kaye. At the conclusion of the dazzling seminar, the bogan remortgages three of its internal organs and part of its McMansion to invest in a yet-to-be-constructed waterfront villa in a part of the Gulf of Carpentaria that is 'about to boom'. This speculatory process is replicated in other emotion-/ego-driven acquisitions in its home town, all highly leveraged.

This complete lack of portfolio diversification leaves the bogan's nascent empire open to xtreme things. When property prices increase, it will take out a high-interest equity loan against its existing properties to fund the acquisition of new ones, further outsmarting the market with its inspired blend of greed and hubris. Feeling every bit the bulletproof oligarch, it will purchase things such as high-performance vehicles, yachting holidays and a home theatre system the size of Barnaby Joyce's economic incompetence. Disappointed that the 'HEHEHE' personalised numberplate is not available, it settles for 'NVESTA'.

A year or two down the track, the federal government reluctantly accepts that it can no longer fund policies designed to artificially inflate residential property values and appease gluttonous bogan voters. Prices then fall moderately, sending the bogan's bloated and astoundingly leveraged portfolio into a tailspin. The bank then calls in some negative equity loans and the bogan is forced to arrange a string of hasty auctions at the bottom of the market. All that remains is a five-year-old car, a five-year-old TV and a bank account the size of Peter Garrett's project management skills. As the bogan dejectedly sifts through its mail on auction day, it eyes a pamphlet guaranteeing 30% returns on the stock market and an accompanying seminar at a nearby motel the following weekend.

Their taxpayer dollars

The bogan hates tax. It will go to remarkable lengths to concoct a system of cash jobs, shifty accountants and bald-faced lies in order to minimise the amount of money that it contributes to sustain the nation of which it is so proud. However, when political correctness goes mad, the nanny state will often catch the bogan out and make it pay something approximating a fair amount of tax. After briefly considering getting Slater & Gordon to take their case to the Maxtreme Court, the bogan realises that cooperating with the intellectuals at the Australian Taxation Office is not as horrifying as it initially thought.

Now that the bogan has paid some tax, it is entitled to demand (via its trusted news sources) that the entire federal budget is dedicated solely to bankrolling boganity. The bogan is not racist, but a government plan to spend millions of the bogan's taxpayer dollars on getting Aboriginal life expectancy to within ten years of the rest of Australia is unacceptable to the non-Aboriginal bogan. This stance is confirmed later that night, when the bogan sees a cheerful Ernie Dingo in perfect health on its plasma screen. At this point, the bogan will announce to the others in the room that the government does indeed need to be sacked.

But it's not just that bogans want the federal budget to be entirely geared towards bogans; each bogan wants the budget to be all about its own agenda for the coming months. This can range from demands to inexplicably double the baby bonus (despite its bumper sticker vowing that Australia is full), crank up the first homeowner's grant to exacerbate an asset bubble, or reward a moronic Facebook group that wants another one-off $900 just because. They're the bogan's taxpayer dollars, dammit, and the bogan wants them returned to its bank account in exponential quantities.

While the bogan has no concept of the administrative and other costs of running a first world democracy, it has an intuitive sense of when it is being ripped off. The stamp duty on its McMansion is absurdly high, and it's definitely not related to the enormous infrastructure expense of yet another sprawling and inefficient housing estate on the urban fringe, subsidised by non-bogans. The bogan's taxpayer dollars demand a train, a school, and Krispy

Kreme within a three-minute drive of wherever it chooses to construct its 40-square glass cube. And the first homeowner's grant should be extended to all homeowners to instantly make homes cheaper. And now that there's no remaining agricultural land within 70 kilometres of a capital city, food is too expensive. The bogan's taxpayer dollars require that the government 'does something' that allows the bogan to continue existing entirely separately from the consequences of its actions.

Cheap petrol

It emerges from its cave. Primed for a successful hunt, the patient bogan is aware that it can sometimes take hours to find its desired prey. It searches down in the valleys and up on the hilltops, eyes alert, scanning the landscape, limbs supple, ready to spring. Despite countless potential distractions, the bogan remains focused. By now the sun is high in the sky and the bogan is becoming thirsty. Up ahead, it sees something, half-obscured by a bush, shimmering in the heat haze. Could it be what the bogan has searched so hard for? The bogan reaches for its weapon, and with adrenaline coursing through its veins, it sees that its four-cents-off-fuel docket is still within its use-by date. The bogan pounces.

Petrol is more important to the bogan than anything else. A one cent rise in the price of petrol will cost the bogan numerous cents per week. Cents that could be used purchasing a vehicle with a more maxtreme fuel-swigging engine, or on upgrading to an even more grotesque McMansion ten kilometres further from its workplace. While the bogan is perfectly happy to spend alarming amounts of money on anything Harvey Norman is offering interest-free, domestically produced foreign label beer, or whatever Christian Audigier is foisting on it this season, subtle movements in the price of fuel induce a level of horror equivalent to that produced by multiple current affairs program segments running on multiple channels simultaneously.

The field of boganomics is a landmine-strewn paddock with no defined boundaries, no farmer, and a mob of rabid beasts headbutting each other intermittently. While the bogan has a vague awareness that petrol prices are the Arabs' fault, it also knows that it's the government's fault. The greedy oil companies also get a healthy slice of the bogan's blame. It's certainly not the fault of the bogan's penchant for energy consumption, or the economics of the earth's geology. All that the bogan needs to know is that it's getting ripped off, and wants justice. The kind of justice that delivers unto the bogan an endless stream of awesome, while simultaneously ensuring there are no consequences for its cretinous actions.

After idling in a queue for ten minutes, the bogan's patriotic Chevrolet contains an extra 30 litres of fuel. As the proud bogan strides towards the counter, it knows that its financial prudence, along with its lengthy suburban hunt, has saved it over a dollar. But pride leads to complacency. The bogan's previously steely focus is scuttled by the drinks fridge to the left, and the magazine rack to the right. It is reminded of its thirst. Ninety seconds later, it waddles out clutching to its chest the massive cans on the front of a $6 lad's magazine, and two massive cans of Mother.

Buying Australian made
As has been sufficiently covered hereabouts, the bogan likes things. Particularly compelling to the bogan are things it can buy. Big things, flashy things with mysterious properties, interest-free things, things

powered by petrol, and even things that aren't things. Following a concerted campaign by the Australian Chamber of Commerce and Industry, the bogan believes that it can also buy its kids a job. While the bogan has little interest in retraining itself or carrying out unpleasant tasks like driving taxis full of other drunken bogans, it nonetheless clings ardently to the idea that it always deserves a job, no matter what. As a result, it wants Indians to stop taking its job, and keenly awaits the invention of a driverless taxi.

To the bogan, buying Australian made is the retail equivalent of wearing a flag cape and punching on at the Big Day Out. That is to say, totally maxtreme true blue. It's what the ANZACs would have done, had they not purchased British Lee-Enfield rifles for their victory at Gallipoli instead. In its generous attempts to buy its kids a job, the bogan will even buy as many Australian made houses as its pyramid-scheme-wary bank manager will allow it to, meaning that its kids will indeed have to work numerous jobs to ever be able to buy into the bogan-bloated property market.

With its canny, job-buying real estate investments in place, the bogan knows that it can add value to each property by making improvements to them. Off to Bunnings Warehouse the bogan will march, to buy as many water features, bathroom cabinets and stainless steel splashbacks as its third credit card will permit. Thanks to Bunnings' buying power, the bogan can secure more Chinese-made products for its buck than ever before. As it turns out, while the bogan is fiercely vocal about buying Australian made, it is ultimately a short-sighted, self-interested cretin more interested in out-glitzing its neighbours. Any attempt to explain this to the bogan will result in glassing with a Russian-made IKEA tumbler that costs only $1.49 each.

Indeed, while the bogan seems quite content to have its personal purchasing decisions expedite the collapse of the Australian automotive, textiles, clothing and footwear, and tyre manufacturing industries, it reserves the right to complain. Whenever a factory closure is announced, it will shout at its Japanese plasma TV for Kevin Rudd/Julia Gillard/Mark Latham or whoever is leading the ALP when this book goes to print to 'do something'. Its national duty thus served, the bogan will change the channel in time for *Two and a Half Men*, thus buying Charlie Sheen's ex-wife's lawyer a job.

Banks

The bogan will tell you that banks are greedy, evil institutions run by corporate fat cats and con men. But in 2009, the average Australian bogan willingly gave at least 10% of its disposable income to banks and other providers of consumer credit. The bogan does not extend this kind of generosity to any other group, proving that despite often bleating to the contrary regarding profiteering, hidden fees and other rip-offs on *Today Tonight* and *A Current Affair*, bogans like banks.

This contradictory behaviour is typical of the bogan, and is driven by some of the bogan's primordial likes: owning things, big things (and therefore owning big things), along with its inability to think beyond the next ad break in *Two and a Half Men*, which renders incomprehensible the concept of saving. This means that in order to own big things, the bogan must find someone else to pay for them. Enter banks. Bank executives, rivalling Max Markson in the evil genius stakes, have long known that the bogan is incapable of turning down even the most draconian, financially crippling loan agreement in order to acquire a bigger house, car, television and ride-on lawn mower than its neighbour.

While the bogan will cry foul when its credit becomes more expensive or financing is denied, and the bank will respond quoting wholesale funding costs or default rate statistics, this type of exchange can be likened more to a lover's tiff than any deep-seated hatred – on the part of the bogan at least. Deep down the bogan knows that its love for, and dependence on, its bank is never ending; life simply would not be worth living without the tender touch of finance that allows it to partially own such a vast array of objects.

It is a match made in heaven. The bogan: hunter gatherer of consumer goods, provider of interest payments. The bank: able to satisfy the bogan's deepest desires with the gentle caress of a rubber stamp between the sheets of its loan application form.

Low interest rates

The bogan understands economics. With a level of understanding akin to James Cameron's grasp of screenplays, the bogan will frequently invoke its right to free speech to opine vociferously on the performance of the economy, thus the performance of the government of the moment. And the bogan knows that there is only one true measure of economic performance: interest rates.

Interest rates are the Reserve Bank's sole means of regulating an overinflating economy, or spurring on sluggish consumer and business spending by discouraging or encouraging bank lending. However, unlike 'conventional' economic wisdom, which the bogan is assured by News Ltd is spurious, the bogan knows that a truly strong economy exists only when interest rates are at all-time record lows. The bogan approaches interest rates much like a climatologically paranoid beaver. Should it rain heavily, the beaver's dam could well be fucked. The bogan, loaded up with $500,000 of borrowed money to pay off the McMansion, views rising interest rates much like incoming inclement weather – that is, a clear signal of impending economic doom.

Thus, every month, there is a near-pornographic obsession in the trashmedia with the upcoming announcements on interest rates, as 'journalists' rapidly calculate the monthly cost facing the overleveraged bogan's average mortgage repayments. Accordingly, bogans will express outrage when the banks have the temerity to 'pass on the rate rise'. National politicians will then fuel the flame of righteous bogan fury, claiming that the banks have a responsibility to bogans everywhere, and that their behaviour (making a profit) is un-Australian.

Once the dust has settled, the bogan will begin complaining to everyone about how the rising interest rates are the government's and the banks' fault, and that they are now in 'mortgage stress', because that is a term they heard Kochie use once. This is despite the fact that at the time of writing mortgage rates are still about half the level they were in 1991. This is also despite the fact that the bogan has happily loaded up the credit card at 20% for a new bookshelf from IKEA. Still, a 0.25% increase in the interest rate is enough to send the bogan into a seething rage.

The bogan, under the extraordinary levels of mortgage stress it inherited due to the policies of a government that has no control over interest rates, will approach the bank, asking to fix its exchange rate. It understands economics, but not fixed or variable mortgages. It resigns itself to watching the monthly announcement on the increase in interest rates, and will then exercise its right to free speech to opine vociferously about how unaffordable housing is in Australia.

Playing the market

The bogan's love of making a quick buck is well noted, so it was only a matter of time before it turned its Lilliputian attention span to the sharemarket and its promise of easy, maxtreme wealth. But the bogan isn't interested in investing. It doesn't care for fundamental analysis, P/E ratios or portfolio diversification. Even the shortest investment horizon is too far by half. The bogan wants a quick fix, a super expressway to leviathan plasmas, hot Asian escorts and solid gold houses.

Taking Kochie's advice on *Sunrise*, the bogan puts $5000 in a managed fund. But after a year, the bogan is shocked to learn the fund has only made a paltry 12% (despite outperforming the market by 4%). It had expected to turn that $5000 into at least $100,000 by now!

The exasperated bogan then accompanies its entrepreneurial mate Troy to a seminar that promises retirement by forty. The bogan loves being in on a secret, and the seminar seems to offer an exclusive avenue to intense max millions. Two hours later, however, the bogan exits the seminar hungry, confused and dissatisfied: the free sushi had weird seafood in it, it doesn't understand what a CFD is, and the only time it had ever been exposed to a stop order in the past was when it attempted to enter its partner's back door without prior permission. Besides, the promised 25% per annum return is still grossly inadequate.

Its plans of becoming the next Warren Buffett buffeted, the bogan considers doubling its money at the dogs when the conversation at Thursday night poker turns to the market. 'Boys,' the bogan's business mate Troy says to the attentive crowd, 'a mate of mine gave me a hot tip . . .' Scrambling outside in between Coronas, the bogan jumps on the iPhone to his wife. 'Jade, we're gonna be rich,' he exhorts excitedly. 'Can you free up some money . . .'

The next day, the bogan puts the children's education fund in Yam Aha Ltd, a highly leveraged agricultural investment scheme, growing yams in Papua New Guinea with revolutionary farming techniques. Not content with the promised 150% return, the bogan then takes out a margin loan, boosting his surefire, guaranteed return to a whopping 300%.

Initially the stock does well, prompting the bogan to gloat to his friends about 'playing the market' and to purchase a new jet ski and 3D plasma. One month later the stock has turned south as Tropical Cyclone Wilson leaves the summer yam harvest in ruins, and the bogan yammering. Initially, the bogan slogs it out like an ANZAC, taking solace in Troy's sage forecast that the world price of yams is about to rocket as the Chinese government produces ethanol from yam extract. The next month, however, the stock plummets before going into a trading halt as ASIC announces Yam Aha is really a front for endangered parrot smugglers.

Forced to sell the McMansion to meet the margin call, the bogan vows to be wiser with his money in future. Until Troy tells him about the octagon scheme . . .

The casino

For the male bogan, failure is not an option. Until it fails. Until then, anything the bogan applies its formidable frontal lobe to will result in maxtreme success, monetary gain and a bevy of fecund teenage nubiles waiting in the harem. The simplest, most effective, surefire means of success is winning money purely by applying its savant-like statistical skills to the art of gambling and winning heaps of cash. And the place it can do that, while nestled in the cocoon of a room full of other bogans, is the casino.

The Casino represents everything the bogan likes, wants, aspires to and fails at. An enormous glitzy shortcut of a metropolis that promises instant riches, human peacocks, velvet ropes, year-long Cirque du Soleil (or other franchised entertainment), bad nightclubs and, of course, lots and lots of shopping. Often emblazoned with a title like 'The Entertainment Capital of the World', it is a schmaltzy nod to the depravity that is the ectoplasm of the bogan city. Every major city has a casino, and bogans will drive for upwards of 100 kilometres to arrive at its shining temple to mediocrity.

Here, the bogan can apply its skills as an uninformed gambler to its heart's content, on a variety of games, from cards, to spinning wheels, to computers with fixed odds. Of 87%. Poker machines, beloved of bogans and elderly folk everywhere, are an incredible example of the mind-boggling mathematical ineptitude of the bogan. For every dollar that gets put into poker machines in a given state, they will return as little as 69 cents. Yet still, the bogan knows it will 'beat the house'. It knows this because it once saw an episode of *Las Vegas*, where an affable simpleton overcame insurmountable odds through simple persistence and self-belief and won a million dollars. Characteristically, however, it failed to realise the distinction between what it sees on television and how it lives its life. Life imitating crap art. The bogan doesn't care for Oscar Wilde, so heads for the counter to get more dollar coins. This could very well be its lucky day.

CELEBRITIES

Velvet ropes

Despite its loud, yowling denial of this fact to any bouncer who glances in its direction, the bogan loves to queue. Nightclub operators have been aware of this for many years, and prime bogan clubbing localities are famous for creating ten-metre queues at the front door of a half-empty bar. The queuing process creates anticipation in the bogan's mind, like a particularly fastidiously wrapped gift.

Often, though, a queue of bogans will become unruly. Forced to arrange themselves in a logical sequence, squabbles and yelling matches regularly erupt, creating a public nuisance and causing the venue operator to worry about being placed in a 'high risk' liquor licence category. The solution for this problem is a velvet rope.

Put a velvet rope anywhere, and the bogan will line up behind it. It will queue for longer periods, and with less complaint, than it will behind a rope of any other fabric, alloy or fibre. The presence of velvet is almost soothing to the bogan, and brings forth some of its best behaviour. But there are other motivators behind this improved etiquette, for the bogan is a complex beast.

Because the rope is velvet, the bogan will assume that whatever it is excluding people from is VIP, and likely to contain a DJ. Or *celebrities*. There could even be maxtreme danger. Either way, a velvet rope makes the bogan strangely docile when it eventually gets to the front of the queue and is informed that it will cost $50 to proceed further. It will obediently hand a pineapple to the cosmetics-smeared door wench operating the till.

Once inside, the bogan will eagerly scan the room, searching for more velvet ropes. There is one by the cloak room, so the bogan joins this queue. Fifteen minutes later, jacket offloaded for

$5, the bogan is ready to queue for a $9 bottle of locally produced foreign label beer, or a $10 Breezer. It will spend the remainder of the night switching between the bar queue and the velvet rope in front of the DJ booth, where it attempts to grind hips with inebriated bogans of the opposite sex each time the smoke machine creates enough haze to lend the air of initial mystique.

The bogan emerges from the club at 4 am, $200 poorer, and visibly irritated due to the queue at the cab rank being framed only by a sticky steel rail.

Reality TV

The bogan has always been misunderstood. Sick of being told by scathing blogs that it is not inspired, talented and of immense value to the nation, it simmers on its lounge suite, plotting its revenge. It sees no real difference between its clueless, indolent self and the people that it sees on the red carpet. The bogan is of the opinion that years of hard work, skill and sacrifice aren't really the key things behind success . . . all that is really required is for the bogan to loudly announce a desire to be a celebrity.

For years, this didn't work. The bogan's closest approximation to fame was the time it was at the same petrol station as Red Symons, and its television screen remained filled with people whose talent and work ethic was far in excess of its own. This changed for good in 1992, when *Sylvania Waters* hit Australian TV screens. The unscripted show followed a family of newly cashed-up bogans who spent and bickered their way through six months of existence. The bogan viewers were transfixed: 'I love spending and arguing!' said the uninteresting bogan. 'I should be on telly too!'

The floodgates were open. TV executives realised that not only did the bogan want to watch other bogans doing nothing in particular, they would also climb over each other to be on these shows free of charge. A televisual nosedive of low cost, low value programming ensued, with advertisers realising that reality TV had herded the most easily brainwashed segment of Australia into a paddock 30 minutes wide.

By the turn of the century, the pinnacle of mediocre reality television had appeared. After passionately pitching their bogan quirks at the show's producers, a dozen or so bogans were locked in a camera-riddled house at Dreamworld and subjected to various pointless and temporary scenarios for the vicarious amusement of the bogans back home. It constituted irrefutable evidence to the bogan that it was worthy of celebrity status, which compelled it to behave accordingly, whether it had been on television or not. Big Brother alumni then go on to bigger and better things, like Hotdogs' *Up-Late Game Show*.

Some analysts thought reality TV would be a brief fad, but they failed to understand the bogan's bottomless need for validation and glitz. As a result, bogans now watch competitions like: fat bogans dieting, tone deaf bogans wailing, hungry bogans cooking, clumsy bogans dancing, and bogan scrags being transformed into bogan scrags in evening dresses. And because it's bogan versus bogan, the bogan always wins.

P!nk

Alecia Moore first entered the Australian consciousness a decade ago, with an R&B-by-numbers single called 'There You Go', in whose video she rode around on a motorbike and gave bad girl attitude to an X-boyfriend. The bogan liked this, and propelled it to #2 on the Australian singles charts. It was just the beginning. Since then, Pink has had an additional *twelve* solo singles chart in the Australian top seven, but only three in her native USA. So what's she been doing that gets the antipodean bogan so damn enthused? Shitloads.

Pink met her husband (a motocross racer) at the 2001 X Games, and has since acquired the ability to ride motorbikes. She used this skill to woo prime bogan love-object Rove McManus, allowing a national TV audience to witness her teaching Rove how to be xtreme. Rove reciprocated by fawning shamelessly and exhorting his audience to supply Pink with their bogan bucks. Pink speaks the bogans' language. She rebelled against conventional literacy and social norms by titling her second album *M!ssundaztood*, and regularly spells her stage name 'P!nk'. The bogan appreciates the gesture, as it considers itself m!ssundaztood also, LMAO.

Primarily, Pink's marketing strategists target teenage female bogans, with a defiant message of how unique and uncontrollable she is. The teenage female bogan empathises with this message, and is controlled by the marketers into buying yet another concert ticket, and buying yet another album to be unique, just like the other individuals in Pink's target demographic who have sent the thing 10 × platinum. P!nk (LOL) undertakes stadium tours of Australia every seven minutes, allowing the fans to always have something new to purchase. Until the show ended this was always accompanied by another spruiking visit to her favourite little buddy on Channel 10. Then, as the adult femme-bogan wants nothing more than to be a teenage femme-bogan again, they embrace P!nk with a similarly slavish enthusiasm, waxing lyrical over how 'cool' and 'empowering' she is, effectively demonstrating how tenuous their grasp of those words was.

In the same way that the bogan trusts Pink with its money, it also trusts her as a source of both domestic and foreign political knowledge. The bogan's knowledge of international relations was augmented by her track 'Dear Mr President', which commandeered populist anti-Bush sentiments. She also (on behalf of animal welfare advocates PETA) lectured the Australian wool industry on the practice of mulesing. She later admitted that her position was 'bullshit', saying, 'I probably could have done a lot more [research]'. The bogan forgave her public misinformation campaign, because she was 'so real'.

Five albums in, she toured Australia again in 2009, selling over 650,000 tickets, mainly to bogans. Her ability to fleece the bogan had become unsurpassed – topping John Farnham's Whispering Jack tour for the most Australian shows in a tour, including a record 17 shows at Melbourne's Rod Laver Arena. What could possibly be left for greedy Alecia's bogan cash vacuum? Her management pondered this and eventually found the answer. She has recently signed a three-year contract to be the face of V8 Supercars (the trans-generational bogan institution), including a special effects-laden TV commercial. A commercial that features her baring her midriff, chomping down on an entirely non-phallic sausage, falling into the arms of a big, strong V8-man, readjusting her breasts and verbally abusing a midget. The very embodiment of female bogan empowerment. That's right, not content to surpass Farnsey in ticket sales, she's decided to go after his rusted-on baby boomer audience, and cannibalise him completely. He'll be tickled pink.

Red carpet specials

This could so easily have been about the bogan love of awards
ceremonies. Awards ceremonies are, by and large – in the bogan
mind – celebrations of famous people being xtremely good at
being famous. Hour after hour of recognisable people reading
off a teleprompter about how good these famous people are at
the primacy of bogan pursuits – sport (watching), television, film
and bad music – seems to be audiovisual crack for most bogans.
At least, judging by the audience that tunes in to the Logies each
year it is.

But it would be wrong to suggest that the bogan simply loves
awards ceremonies. TV networks have figured out that, like T20
cricket, Slamball, *Underbelly*, megachurches and Ministry of
Sound, taking things bogans like, removing the boring bits and
repackaging them as separate products often results in an orgiastic
bogan spending or viewing spree of epic proportions. So, with
awards ceremonies, all reference to the pursuit being awarded is
removed, and two hours are dedicated to watching people arrive
at a party.

Thus, the bogan female can indulge in her perceived love
of couture, commenting snidely on other bogan females who
managed to finagle themselves a spot in front of a television
camera. That these briefly famous bogans are wearing clothes
that are likely to wind up on the racks of bogan stores in various
iterations in the coming months is of no concern to the bogan of
course, who is apparently incapable of thinking beyond the two-
hour red carpet special. Meanwhile, the male bogan has an ideal
opportunity to scope some massive cans.

Another common theme to the red carpet special is the presence of an individual for whom there is no rational explanation. That they exist at all is baffling in the xtreme. That they are apparently beloved of bogans is confusing to the point of aneurism. They have been on television seemingly forever, and often have not altered in appearance in that time. Their hair hovers nebulously in that unique TV-land purgatory between wig, actual hair and strange lacquered helmet. And the granddaddy of all of these is Richard Wilkins. Whether or not he is real is up for furious debate. He may be a bogan construct. But, along with the likes of Daryl Somers, Sonia Kruger, Karl Stefanovic, David 'Kochie' Koch and Kerri-Anne Kennerley, he is a predominantly synthetic, vacant shell into which the bogan can pour their personality assumptions: a nice, white, inoffensive head attached to a microphone.

At the end of the ceremony, the bogan goes to sleep. Upon waking, it scans the paper or news website for photos of the ordeal . . .

Max Markson

Despite his x-enabled name and vast bogan-derived riches, Max Markson remains a mysterious figure to bogans. Primarily famous for being near other famous people, Markson differs from the rather pointless Richard Wilkins because the former is an evil genius. Wilkins, on the other hand, is alleged to be some form of polymer that derives sustenance from nutrients found in red coloured carpet, and the shiny leather cladding Max Markson's feet.

Markson is a 'talent agent' and publicist who is notable for exploiting other people's mediocre fame, and he specialises in trying to grind out 15 and a half minutes of fame for bogans such as Tania Zaetta (military sex scandal), Pauline Hanson (political sex scandal), and Susie Maroney (criminal sex scandal). At the time of writing, the headline on his website (www.marksonsparks.com.au) is 'Lara Bingle signs with Markson Sparks!', while the second news item is 'Ed Hardy joins Markson Sparks!'. Within a week of Bingle signing with his agency, there happened to be a front page sports sex scandal involving Bingle. His hypnotic control over the bogan's media needs is just that strong.

But there's STILL more. Tim Shaw from Demtel is a Markson client, as is Catriona Rowntree, (and now here's . . .) Moira, a Daddo, and the entire cast of the 2008 series of *The Biggest Loser*. Markson defies every medical and financial principle to keep these careers alive. It is not known whether he uses black magic, an elaborate system of ropes and pulleys, or incomprehensibly large bribes funded by corruption in war-torn Third World nations.

Markson is on the record as saying 'I can make anyone a star', which is immensely reassuring to bogans, who want very badly to be stars. The bogan seems to have decided that its chances of becoming a Markson-conjured celebrity are immeasurably increased by rabidly consuming whatever antimatter bilge that Markson Sparks is pumping into magazines at the time. It is almost certain that a sex scandal involving both Lara Bingle and Christian Audigier will occur in the next three minutes.

Forgiving celebrities

Readers of this book would be excused for thinking that the bogan lacks a central nervous system and is utterly incapable of remorse or forgiveness. While that assumption is fundamentally correct, there have been a few sightings of bogan compassion. One of the most intriguing among these is the bogan's ability to forgive misbehaving celebrities.

The bogan wants desperately to be a celebrity, but has no particular skill set. The unfortunate truth in this is that 99.9% of them are not celebrities, and due to their lack of any particular talents, nor are they 'celebrities waiting to be discovered'. In the meantime, many among this 99.9% will dedicate significant amounts of time and money to celebrities, either by buying magazines which gossip about celebrities, watching shows which gossip about celebrities, or gossiping about celebrities with other bogans.

The bogan has convinced itself that the worth of a celebrity is entirely dependent on what they, the bogan, think of them at any given time. As such, the bogan has developed detailed (if nonsensical) insights and monologues on dozens of celebrities that it can rattle off at a moment's notice. From time to time, a celebrity does something that will meet with the fearsome wrath of the bogan. The offences can include cheating on a spouse, calling a linesman a 'spastic', lying down on a rowing boat, entering politics, subjecting children to polygraph tests, or wearing a bogan-reviled garment to a red carpet event.

For a period of weeks – or, indeed, months – this celebrity will have gushing torrents of bogan hate pouring down upon it. It will come in the form of spittle-soaked talkback radio rants, fact-orexic magazine exposés, and foodcourt conversations with the capacity to strip bystanders of their will to live. Fortunately for the maligned celebrity in question, there are three ways out.

Firstly, the bogan's Lilliputian attention span means that the grave celeb crime is likely to be forgotten by the time its next movie or album comes out. Second, the celebrity may publicly apologise to the bogan. To all the bogans. Because that's who the celebrity truly wronged, here. Not the cuckolded wife, nor the estranged political movement, but the bogans.

Finally, in the wake of this apology, the bogan can prove to itself that it is a wonderful human being. By mentally extending the olive branch to Tiger Woods when he walks up to a tee, the bogan will feel warm and compassionate. In this moment, the bogan is basically Tiger's best mate, deeply connected to his soul. As Tiger collects the trophy at tournament's end, the bogan can reflect on the roller coaster relationship they had with Tiger, and decide that it's okay. That Tiger, despite his foibles, despite the pain he caused the bogan, is okay.

The Logies

The bogan is furious. *Underbelly* **has been nominated for the 'Most** Outstanding Drama Series' Logie Award. This is wrong, as the bogan knows that the correct category for the show is the 'Most Outstanding Factual Program' Logie. But, being the compassionate bivalve that it is, the bogan is willing to overlook this grave error and watch the awards ceremony anyway. Part of the reason why it still watches is because of its love of the voting process. The Gold Bogie is determined by popular vote via soul-sapping trashmedia appendage *TV Week*. It is understood that 98% of the votes are cast by 13-year-old girls, network publicists and bogans. As a result, it is Australian television's most revered prize.

Local television content laws notwithstanding, the Logie Awards are ample proof that the bogan is a creature that cherishes mediocrity and habit. Intimidated by the prospect of a variety of stars gracing its plasma screen, the bogan will cling needily to the same star for years at a time. Ray Martin won four successive Gold Bogies in the mid-nineties for his bogan-friendly consumer outrage journalism, before Lisa McCune got the next four for keeping Mt Thomas free of ethnic minorities. Georgie Parker pinched the two after that, then Rove got the next three for pandering to foreign entertainers in town on promotional tours. Since then, every Gold Logie has gone to an actor who had constantly been on Australian television for decades.

The annual awards ceremony aspires to be similar to an American awards night, except shitter. In this pursuit of media-ocrity, the bogan summoned Bert Newton to host the 2010 awards. This was primarily due to his proven ability to count backwards from 20, his proven inability to attach fox hide to his cranium, and his rare capacity to incorporate sexual innuendo that is both acceptable and thrilling to grandmothers. Twenty ten is the first time Bert has flown solo in the gig since 1993, demonstrating that network executives were plumbing new unimaginative depths to create an insipid bogan-pacifying lump of pabulum four hours long.

The bogan will watch the program, intent on learning which of its favourite shows and 'personalities' will win its cherished 'Most Popular' awards. It will smile in the satisfied manner of someone who did not submit a vote, so can approve of any selection when Anonymous Blonde takes out Most Popular New Talent for the twelfth year running. The bogan will be well prepared for the main event, having sat through a solid hour of jaw-droppingly stupefying 'repartee' between celebrities with unmoving eyebrows and Richard Wilkins, whose entire being is now 83.6% botulinum toxin. As his radioactive orange skin (made from the same polymer

as Bert's toupée) blends with the crimson of the carpet, bogans will comment to one another just how well he and Rebecca Gibney have aged.

WAGs

At this point it barely requires mentioning that the bogan lusts for celebrity and its trappings with a fervour that would shame the randiest 13-year-old bogan upon the discovery of RedTube. Of course, the bogan is more than happy to live vicariously through those who can achieve fame in their place and sportspeople are among the most prominent of these. They are often local, and are willing to engage in maxtreme behaviour in public which the bogan can be outraged at, then forgive. There is, however, a celebrity that appeals even more greatly to the bogan than the footballer or cricketer. Their girlfriend.

By its early twenties, even the most self-deluded male bogan has reached the conclusion that it is not destined for a lifetime of sporting glory and fawning groupies, instead spending its time at the local footy club drinking Mexican beer with its mates and discussing how awesome it would be for all seven of them to shag one chick.

The femme-bogue, however, has an alternative, one she can cling to for at least another decade. One that is more appealing, as it requires little more effort than the willingness to endure multiple penetrations (anal) from seven smashed athletes. She still has a chance to be a WAG. The WAG is, to the bogan, famous, yet has achieved little, if anything, beyond appearing on the cover of *Zoo Magazine* under the guise of being an Australian cricketer's missus. She has a bloke at her side willing and able to fork over for cosmetic enhancements of all sorts, and actively encourages her desire to paint herself a sinister shade of orange and bare her newly massive cans in the men's magazines or on the red carpet.

Moreover, the WAG has only two genuine obligations: to attend football matches (watching said matches is optional), and stapling an expensive-looking dress covered in sequins to its breasts once a year at the sport's awards night. Beyond this, the WAG can pursue any and all goals it chooses, from hosting a travel show to interviewing other WAGs on the red carpet.

This all culminates in the femme-bogue deciding that becoming a WAG is her calling. Her destiny. It is what she was put on Earth to do. This results in weekly pilgrimages to weekend haunts known for containing athletes, where the femme-bogues stalk their prey with a single-minded, ruthless determination more commonly witnessed among rutting caribou. By the end of the night, the female bogan has passed out in a tangle of arms, legs, sequins and shame and its male counterpart is in hospital, having been glassed in the side of the face by the halfback flanker it thought was hitting on its missus.

Ned Kelly

The self-congratulatory first year Arts student loves the idea of Che Guevara. While Artsy generally knows little about Guevara's murderous ways, it remains thrilled to embrace the stylised logo of this young, attractive rogue who symbolised the liberation of other lefties from things that lefties didn't like. The bogan, on the other hand, is generally unmoved by Guevara, because he was complicated, eloquent (and generally not in English) and un-Australian. Still, the bogan attempted to co-opt this figure, as it saw so many examples of him on brightly-coloured t-shirts. The disturbing predilection of second and third year Arts students to query bogans on who, exactly, that person was, led them to look closer to home for their icons.

Being itself a resourceful student of history, the bogan settled on Ned Kelly as its countercultural pin-up boy. Born into a criminal family in Victoria during the 1850s, young Ned's first brush with the law came at age 14, when he was arrested for assaulting a Chinese farmer. While the bogan generally does not know anything about Ned Kelly other than the fact that it likes him, the bogan would approve of its precocious hero beating up an ethnic minority before he was even able to grow his beard. The following year, Kelly assaulted a bloke who accused his mate of borrowing his horse. The bogan mentally substitutes 'horse' with 'HSV', and approves.

After a prison stint for other HSV-related crimes, Ned won a bare-knuckle fistfight, got arrested for public drunkenness, and ran away from the pigs. Approved. More run-ins with the constabulary followed, leading to Kelly shooting three of them in the bush, and robbing some banks. The pigs arrested and held Ned's mates, to the horror of the bogan. Nothing happened for a year or so, until Ned turned up in Glenrowan, kitted out in his famous iron suit. The bogan mentally substitutes 'iron' with 'lime green polyester', and approves. After taking hostages at the pub, Ned's plan unravelled. The pigs shot Ned in the legs, and his co-conspirators all died. Kelly was hanged in November 1880, although approximately 30,000 of the bogan's ancestors signed a petition to spare his life. The bogan mentally substitutes 'signed a petition' with 'joined a Facebook group', and approves.

The bogan's lack of interest in the details of Kelly's life and death allows it to project onto Kelly anything that it wants. Unionised bogans have conceptually linked him with the Eureka flag, where a six-month-old Ned Kelly is understood to have totally killed some pigs on behalf of his comrades. Other bogans see him as a high-minded Robin Hood, despite the fact that Kelly acted almost exclusively in the interest of his own vanity, prosperity and freedom. Others still see him as a true blue gangsta, yo. The bogan's deep love of quick and easy part-truths, nurtured by *Today Tonight*, allows it to live a life free of any hypocrisy at all. Catering to its market, Australia Post released a Ned Kelly postage stamp to mark the centenary of his death back in 1980. The bogan mentally substitutes 'postage stamp' with 'extreme tattoo on Ben Cousins' stomach', and approves.

CREATIVE ENDEAVOURS

Arbitrary thievery

It all begins with bar mats. Or street signs. Bogans have an enduring love of home decorating and redecorating, and this love manifests itself in strange ways – particularly during bogan nascence. This is when cash-poor bogans resort to theft to attain the things they need, because the absence of anyone willing to pay them for their lack of skills means that they cannot have them. Depressed by the financial constraints of pathological laziness, the newly adult bogan heads to the local pub's uni night (it matters not whether the bogan attends university), already well prepared by imbibing on Woodies or Cruisers, looking to fill the void.

The bogan then spies the aforementioned bar mat. Excitedly stating that 'It'll look mad on the bar that I'm going to build when I move out', these mats are surreptitiously swiped from under the apathetic bartender's nose. Conspiratorially unveiling the stash in a quiet corner of the pub, the bogan gains the approval of its cabal of similarly inebriated comrades, and on the walk home, they decide that their future home bar would be best equipped by pasting the walls with a random variety of street signs, just like the Hog's Breath Cafe. No sooner has the thought entered their head than they are swinging futilely from a lamppost, images of 'Andrew St' signs sitting above their newly installed kegs and taps flashing through their foggy minds.

The illicit thrill of kleptomania lingers through adulthood, although the actual act of theft is often replaced with 'getting a steal' in the form of an interest-free plasma. Stealing things allows the bogan to have things it wants, without having to do anything of substance to achieve it. Seeing the fame of Rebecca Twigley, Lara Bingle and Richard Wilkins, the bogan reaches a trembling hand for the exposed Bacardi spillover protector. By the time parenthood rolls round, many bogans, still trapped in the same existential malaise of insufficient branded luxury, step up to legitimate shoplifting. Like any junkie, the rush gets harder to find, and pint glasses and witches hats lose their lustre, only to be replaced by lifting a singlet from Bardot or Supré. However, it always comes back to bar mats, often resulting in the arrest of a bogan while on holiday in South East Asia.

Painting

There are zero eyewitness accounts of bogans actually painting. In fact, this entire facet of the bogan personality could be consigned to the realm of mythology, were it not for the fact that the bogan continually appears at various events and functions in pants that are splattered with apparently fresh paint. Jeans, tracksuit pants, and even their favourite Melbourne Cup three-piece, it matters not. Immediately before leaving the house, it seems the bogan cannot resist the urge to slap a quick second coat on the pool room's feature wall.

So, while there is no recorded evidence of this behaviour, it is not hard to imagine. The bogan, halfway out the door to head to the nearest former pub/now pizza bar, dressed in its best and brightest. As it goes to close the door, its eyes linger briefly on the tin of Dulux 'Mocha Jellybean', roller and brush nestling comfortably alongside. The bogan pauses, torn, and a brief grimace of indecision passes its otherwise inscrutable features. Then, in a burst of unrestrained energy, the bogan runs back into the room, picks up the brush and, with a song in its heart, gives the wall the extra application it always needed.

Of course, the bogan seems to be quite the joyous home decorator, as the paint splatter is in no way confined to the body's lower half. Travisty t-shirts, while beloved of and hoarded by the bogan, are not immune, and often fall victim to the bogan's uninhibited brush strokes. It is possible that Ed Hardy is so treasured that it is not worn during these impressionist excursions, although it is also possible that it is impossible to tell with the naked eye whether Ed Hardy shirts have fallen victim to excess splashback.

Such remarkable, across-the-board creativity should, of course, be nourished and encouraged. Next time *you* see a bogan walking down the street, having attempted to surreptitiously engage in this secret past time, do not mock it. Merely nod, smile and give that knowing look that says that you know. And it's okay.

Three-Park Superpass!

The Islamic faith has Mecca, the Catholics have the Vatican City, and the fashion world has Milan. Bogan culture, too, has its own site of pilgrimage – a font of boganic purity, gushing forth in plenty all that is boganesque; that place is Queensland's Gold Coast. On the Gold Coast, not so much a city as a holiday resort-cum-shopping mall-cum-vertical retirement village, no sites are more sacred than that juggernaut triumvirate of bogan fun-in-the-sun, Movie World, Sea World and Wet'n'Wild, all covered under the extravagantly priced Three-Park Superpass.* According to the operator, these theme parks are 'a thrill-seekers [sic] paradise'

---

* As much out of malice as commercial imperative, the equally dumb and crass Dreamworld has been excluded from the Superpass, allowing the bogan to wait in yet another endless queue to lodge an irrational complaint then pay more money.

leading us to conclude that thrill-seeker (bogan) heaven involves some combination of getting sunburnt, being ripped off, thrashing your children in public, waiting in queues and having a chuck from a moving vehicle. Let's break this down.

Warner Bros Movie World Movie World touts itself as 'Hollywood on the Gold Coast', but it differs from the real Hollywood in that no movies have actually ever been made there. (*Scooby Doo* and *House of Wax* just don't count; they are unfit for human consumption.) It is a reproduction of the soulless artifice Hollywood is famous for, *sans* any actual motion picture production. A testament to the cynical genius of marketers as much as it is to the bogan's slack-jawed susceptibility to their ruses, Movie World's success lies in combining everything about mass culture which provides such enduring comfort to the bogan, stripping it of any remaining content, and turning it into an xtreme, bowel-loosening thrill ride experience. The bogan loves Movie World because the rides vaguely remind it of a film it once saw cross-marketed on a Happy Meal, but at that point the bogan stops thinking about it, because everything's going really, really fast.

Sea World Sea World, much like that other Queensland nature abomination, Australia Zoo, seems on the surface to be highly educational, but do not be fooled. You will not learn anything about marine life on Bert and Ernie's Island Holiday, or the amazing Jet Rescue Ride, where somehow you can save a sea lion by riding a jet ski, rather than destroying its habitat and disfiguring its progeny, which is what you'd expect to happen. Sea World is truly a magical place where our natural environment meets high-octane fun, and is summarily ground into extinction.

Wet 'n' Wild Seeing as there is no discernible difference between this place and Sea World (apart from the dolphins in the pool having been replaced by yet more dickheads), there is nothing further to add.

Zoo Weekly

For decades, female bogans have happily purchased lifestyle magazines. These publications gave the 1950s housewife new recipes, new things to knit and new ways to grip the shaft of a feather duster. By the 1970s, these magazines had started to change, with an increase in articles about TV shows and movie stars. By the 1990s, the race to the bottom had reached fever pitch, with illicit affairs and celebrity cover-ups competing for the female bogan's dwindling attention span. In the mid nineties, the publishers observed that all they were providing to the female bogan was smut, scandal and sex tips. 'May I suggest that male bogans want these things too,' said one junior publishing executive, observing the convergence of bogan genders.

Ralph, part of the Kerry Packer bogan harvesting empire, arrived on the scene in 1997. It featured scantily clad women on the front and enough sport and smut to convince some of the more progressive male bogans to stop buying *People/Picture* magazine (both Packer enterprises). The other benefit of *Ralph* for the male bogan was that each edition contained a smattering of health/ lifestyle articles that it would never read. These articles made the magazine technically not porn, and female bogan spouses found it more difficult to object to the magazine's presence in the toilet at casa de bogan.

This uneasy truce continued until 2006, when the ultimate bogan male publication appeared on shelves. *Zoo Weekly* does away with any health and wellbeing content, replacing it with additional scantily clad women, and some more articles that valiantly attempt to classify Lara Bingle photo shoots as AFL/cricket news. The magazine has a team of female sex advice columnists dubbed 'The Threesome', which appeals to the male bogan's desire for maxtreme group sex (but with no other blokes, because that'd be gay). It even contains former *Big Brother* contestants as columnists, along with classic bogan beer pit David Boon. None of these columns are more than 200 words in length, due to the bogan's preference for bright colours and silicone breasts over letters and numbers. In 2007 the Packer empire forked out $94 million to acquire *Zoo Weekly* and tap into this pulsating new vein of boganity. Also included in the deal was the acquisition of *Ralph* rival *FHM*.

Zoo Weekly's publisher pitches its bogan audience to advertisers as 'living for the next party, the next gadget, and the next girl', a summary that compelled the bogan's girlfriend to start a loud argument about the ongoing presence of the magazine in its house. Initially, the male bogan conceded. For the next few weeks, the bogan male purchased *Ralph* and tried to convince itself that the volume of tits in there was adequate. Its relationship improved, with the female bogan seemingly oddly grateful that *Ralph* was around, the very publication that it decried only a decade earlier. In March 2010, she sent her man down to the 7-Eleven to purchase a Diet Coke to pair with her bag of lollies. At the drinks fridge, the male bogan spied the promotional placard that would lead to its undoing: '500 ml can of Mother and copy of *Zoo Weekly* for only $6!' His relationship was doomed.

Short courses

The bogan's lizard brain has a powerful need for recognition in all that it does. This is why it will drive its Chevrolet down streets lined with luxury retail outlets, wear seizure-triggering quantities of jewellery, or sport a t-shirt with a tiger biting some sort of skull/ love heart thing. Easier still is to merely *talk* about things that the bogan intends to do, but in reality will almost certainly never do. These include 'going to see the pyramids' (the moment it has enough money to get to Phuket on Jetstar, off it goes), or 'learning how to shred on the axe!' (as soon as it realises that this requires persistence and dedication over some years, it swiftly places the shiny Ibanez in the corner, and scuttles back to Guitar Hero).

While the bogan will rarely end up doing these things, it derives great satisfaction from the statements of surprise or admiration it receives when loudly announcing these hollow intentions to the world. It is in the interests of other bogans to express this enthusiastic surprise, because the other bogans will expect to receive the same reaction when they announce their new plans to master the stock market, lose 20 kilos, or finally move the family to Queensland.

Eventually, though, the pattern of loud claims and no action becomes apparent, even to one with the negligible self-awareness of the bogan. The second quickest and second easiest way for the bogan to medicate this fleeting perspective on itself is to enrol in a short course. Conducted through TAFE colleges, community centres, or other organisations, these courses involve a couple of hundred dollars of the bogan's money and a commitment of one night a week for a month or two. While even this proves to be too much of an ask for some bogans, many manage to make it through. Often, the bogan will draw on skills it developed during high school – coercing more diligent students into granting the bogan the temporary benefits of proper work. Short courses allow the bogan to simultaneously claim the title of 'educated' while remaining staunchly anti-intellectual.

Two months later, the achievement-oriented bogan emerges like a shimmering butterfly from its shabby chrysalis, replete with the knowledge of how to create wonky ceramic bowls which it will solemnly gift to every one of its relatives that Christmas. While the bogan will certainly never make another ceramic bowl after the conclusion of the course, its sense of smugness inexplicably continues for years. If at any point the smugness begins to abate, the bogan will restore it by resorting to the quickest and easiest method – purchasing another self-help book and adding it to their entirely unread collection on the bookshelf.

Fender Stratocasters

Despite having a lifelong, unfulfilled ambition to have sick chops on the guitar, the bogan is generally a novice when it comes to musical instruments. Often, a bogan will consider purchasing a new electric guitar, but guitars cost at least $250, and the fully sick ones can cost as much as a ginormous plasma screen. Besides, generally the bogan's attempts at this sort of thing have been strangely unrewarding. It's a relief, perhaps, that it instead picks up a $100 Guitar Hero guitar to play Epic Leads on its $350 Xbox.

The bogan likes playing Epic Leads because the bogan is on an inexorable quest for maxtreme awesomeness. And in the age of bogan-friendly shredgaming, the inability to play guitar is no obstacle to a bogan proclaiming itself a massive axe god, and talking about melting bulk face on the weekend. With key influences including Wayne, Garth, Bill and Ted, the bogan is ready to enter the halls of rock guitar excellence. And no rock guitar has more bogan cachet than a Fender Stratocaster.

The Fender Stratocaster (or 'Strat' as the bogan will call it, the nickname perhaps implying a bond between the bogan and its instrument) is the world's best known guitar. It is the one guitar the bogan needs to know, which is lucky because the bogan mistakes the names of all the other guitars for cars or strange foreign food. The bogan also likes the Fender Stratocaster because it thinks it's what Slash played, out in front of that church in the desert, wailing out massive chops in 'November Rain'. (It wasn't. Slash only uses a Les Paul, but the bogan doesn't let facts get in the way of its hero worship.)

The bogan loves to hold the exact Strat that it thinks Slash is famous for playing, except maxximised for shredgaming, and nail sophisticated fingering and picking techniques after a few goes. Then after the outro is done, it's straight back with another soaring classic, with the bogan centre stage, playing more Epic Leads. Even when the game throws up some weird poofy music, the bogan still likes playing its Strat. It can just focus on nailing the timing of objects coming down a 3D-looking fretboard, all the time watching an animated muso in tight jeans rock out for maximum crowd points. It is fair to say the bogan doesn't realise the animated muso-hipster probably drinks soy lattes and reads Henry Miller, and idolises its proto-bogan forefather rockers, who actually knew their way around a genuine Fender Stratocaster. That doesn't matter, because when it comes to Fender Stratocasters, the bogan has no complaints. The bogan likes Fender Stratocasters.

History

We're not talking about the Michael Jackson greatest hits record from his pre-paedophilia period, although there's little to dislike about that, save for the teeth-grindingly bad duet with Paul McCartney. No, we're talking about the other history: that is, things that have already happened. But the bogan is not excited by the intrigues of the Prussian court. It will not explore the minutiae of Carthagean naval tactics, nor develop an appreciation for sublime artifacts from the Kingdom of Benin's golden age. The bogan's history doesn't fuck about with such niceties. The bogan's history is about blood, guts, massive swords and glory that lasts throughout the ages. It's about Spartans with immense rigs, and Vikings with horny helmets. Pirate wenches with busts so heaving, the turbulent seas get jealous. History that's pissed off, soaked in blood, and coming at you like a cavalry charge, making your heart pump like five cans of Steven Segal's Lightning Bolt. History to the maxtreme.

Following in the fine French tradition of getting bogans so excited they simultaneously lose control of their bladders and their wallets, Gallic bogan-baiter Robert Hossein is on a winner with *Ben Hur – the Stadium Spectacular*. Clearly bigger than all previous incarnations of itself, this incredible stadium adaptation of the historically woeful but completely thrilling Hollywood epic starring Charlton Heston is soon to explode into Sydney's ANZ Stadium like a 200 megaton, bogan-homing warhead. According to the website, it 'combines the scale of the Sydney Olympic Games Opening Ceremony with the drama of the slave who dared defy the Roman Empire'. This high-octane gonad-history thrill ride will feature a Roman galleon and a 32-chariot race, fulfilling the history quota but remaining suitably reminiscent of Easternats, with a slightly higher possibility of violent rioting and the rim-looting hijinks.

The website taunts bogans that it is for two nights only, and may possibly arrange exclusive presale tickets to avoid missing out, but chances are this thing will be bum-rushed by so many bogans that the organisers will fear a bogan revolt, and promise to extend the run until it rivals André Rieu's latest marathon tour of Australian scout halls. For when the bogan can get its history served up with enormous explosions, megalitres of blood and huge guns, when it can watch chariots with spinning blades on their rims doing massive burnouts *live on stage*, all while drinking overpriced mid-strength beer out of a plastic cup, the bogan is a slavering demon for history.

Perspective-based photos at famous landmarks

'Wait . . . move ya left hand over a bit . . . that's it . . . nah, wait, ya missed it. Fuck. Try again.'

Travel to any part of the world with any landmark that has appeared in a James Bond movie or a Contiki catalogue, and you will undoubtedly hear words to this effect. With a strong Australian dollar, cheap flights, and internet accommodation bookings, the newly internationalised bogan has embraced overseas trips/tours/drinking with a previously unseen fervour. They then decide, in their uncommonly belated manner, that it would be totally bitchin' if they posed alongside a famous landmark, employing their unparalleled grasp of telephoto perspective to create the impression they're, you know, holding it up! While the bogan has precious little perspective on life, empathy, culture and modesty, it has an unlimited desire for perspective in its photography.

How artistic and clever it makes the bogan feel to have come up with such a devastatingly effective photo. The several hundred other travelling bogans undertaking the same process within a 50 metre radius are clearly ripping off what is an original idea. It is inconceivable that anyone other than that one particular bogan could have realised how extreme it would be if a photo made the Eiffel Tower look really small, with the tip being squeezed by the oily pincers of the bogan.

After the magic of the digital camera allows the bogan to make the requisite 300 attempts to place the photo's two subjects in harmonious alignment, it can be taken home, enlarged 100 times and placed on the wall of the formal living room. The roaring success of the photo is enough to induce the bogan to tell its friends that it's thinking of becoming a pro photographer. Indeed, the possibility of taking more perspective-based photos (along with V Australia now flying to North America) may lure the bogan to journey to NYC to create a sidesplittingly unprecedented scene wherein the Statue of Liberty gets sodomised from behind. An alternative and equally appealing option is to kiss the Sphinx, and then make a joke about getting older pussy. Or, or, what about one where it looks like the ruins of the Acropolis are getting stomped on?!

The bogan will never, ever, ever tire of this.

Bunnings Warehouse

The bogan will tell you that it knows what it wants, but Bunnings disagrees. This is the reason why, when the bogan male heads off at his partner's insistence to purchase new washers for the en suite taps, it will return home two hours later unexpectedly bearing twelve other items that would be of use in projects that the bogan had no prior plans of undertaking. The bogan will not use 90% of these items. Ever. But thanks to the bogan matadors in Bunnings' head office, it will remain convinced that it has purchased well.

Bunnings has been in the hardware business for many decades, and gradually acquired various smaller hardware chains over the years with limited fanfare. The bogan's attention was gained in the mid-nineties, when the first Bunnings Warehouse was opened in the western suburbs of Melbourne. This warehouse was a traditional hardware store, but on hyper maxtreme steroids of insane power. Far larger than a supermarket, the bogan was lured in by thousands of products it didn't need or want, at prices it was ill-equipped to resist. The prices are largely thanks to everything being made in China, which the hyper-patriotic bogan is happy to overlook in order to secure a three-in-one bathroom heater for only $138. Indeed, the emergence of a Bunnings Warehouse within ten kilometres of any McMansion has been a key driver of demand for monstrous garages. The bogan's steadfast belief that bigger is always better means that it sees no problem with this situation.

Bunnings produces multiple catalogues and television commercials per month, which are jammed into letterboxes and plasma screens nationwide. Despite the massive expense of doing this, Bunnings has developed a simplified four-colour catalogue style with black and white sketches of the products instead of photos. This (despite the full-colour printing on parts of most pages) convinces the bogan that it is truly a warehouse, with hardcore savings on catalogue costs reflected in the hardcore prices. The TV commercials feature nasal and functionally illiterate

Bunnings employees, allowing the bogan to feel a sense of human affinity with a chain that netted around $250 from every man, woman and child in Australia in 2008–09.

It is certain that this figure would fall if the bogan ever managed to gain control of its impulses, but fortunately for Bunnings, this is unlikely ever to happen. If it does, Bunnings will put on a sausage sizzle, advertise a 25 cc petrol hedge trimmer in black and white for only $269, and put the bogan right back to square one. In the meantime, the unused 18 square metres of timber decking that the bogan impulse purchased on its last Bunnings visit rots in a pile in the backyard. Its $3.95 Bunnings tarpaulin has long since been relocated to partly cover the rusting (thrice used) 18-burner BBQ with side burner, wok cooker, warming rack, rotisserie and teppanyaki hotplate.

CULTURAL PURSUITS

Books – but only after the movie comes out

Bogans will tell you that they love to read. This is convenient, as reading is, by its very nature, a solitary exercise. As books are generally read away from the presence of other people, it is quite simple to assume the mien of intelligence, and opine solemnly on the quality of either the latest bestseller or a well-known classic without ever actually having moved beyond the blurb. However, in conducting this kind of surreptitious deception, the bogan leaves itself open to exposure – if a comrade has read the book in question and calls the bluff.

As such, the bogan is far more inclined to wholeheartedly embrace the release of books which have subsequently been turned into major motion pictures. *The Power of One, Harry Potter, The Da Vinci Code/Angels and Demons,* the *Twilight* series (oh god, the *Twilight* series – now officially a 'saga'), *The Bourne Identity/ Supremacy/Ultimatum, Memoirs of a Geisha, Silence of the Lambs, Confessions of a Shopaholic, The Devil Wears Prada,* and of course everything by Tom Clancy, John Grisham and Michael Crichton.

An interesting offshoot of this phenomenon is that many bogans actually wind up reading the books in question as they discover – to their own surprise and amazement – that reading can be an edifying experience. This, of course, leads to the natural point at which the bogans resume their pompous proclamations about the book, but now it is only to boldly, lamely state that it is 'way better than the movie'.

This is a ruse, as no bogan worth their salt would willingly sit through all 13,000 pages of the sixth Harry Potter instalment without the film to act as their equivalent of a study guide. That imagination shit's overrated anyway. More sophisticated bogans have, by the way, graduated beyond such primitive options, having discovered Wikipedia, allowing them to look up the synopsis of any book they like, preparing them to pretend that they have read almost anything they like.

However, no one – not even the most late-adopting, slogan-wearing bogan, would ever touch the novelisation of a film. That would be going too far.

André Rieu

André is not the first of his kind – indeed, the bogan was charmed 15 years ago by Vanessa-Mae, an attractive young violinist who plonked techno beats over Bach, Classical Gas, and some other stuff. She went on to cultivate xtremeness by playing on a Prince project titled 'Xpectation'. Her ability to cater to the ADHD market's desire to seem sophisticated was successful, thus setting her up for life.

In a provincial town in the Netherlands, meanwhile, a middle-aged man was surfing the internet and saw what Vanessa-Mae had done. 'I wish to extract much cash money from the bogan also,' he said to himself, 'but how can I do this when I am not a sultry young woman?' André pondered this further, and clicked his clogs together with glee when he realised that there might just be a way. 'Am I not a slightly rogue looking, well dressed gent with a regional orchestra and a cynical mind?' André muttered to nobody in particular. With no responses forthcoming, he interpreted the answer to be in the affirmative.

And, for better or worse, right he was. After a few years of flitting here and there, André Rieu became aware of how to charm the Australian bogan female into revealing to him the soft pink lips of its purse. He pairs his own appeal to middle-aged bogan females with that of an attractive young female soprano singer in his live performances, reducing the resistance of the bogan male to grant his wife the expensive wish of attending one of Rieu's stadium shows. André depicts his critics as members of a stuffy musical elite with narrow aesthetic tastes, which the bogan gratefully assimilates into its own resentment of ambitious people who do not wish to be bogans.

Being aware of the bogan's reluctance to dwell too long on foreign music pieces it is not already familiar with, André intersperses his Australian shows with sing-along favourite tunes such as *Burke's Backyard*, *Bananas in Pyjamas* and *Neighbours*. Indeed, he even guest-starred on *Neighbours* in April 2009, bringing his brand name to the unwashed masses when they least expected it. He released a schmaltzy localised grab for the bogan female's affections in the lead-up to Mother's Day 2008, with *Waltzing Matilda* getting to #1 on the album charts.

While a competent musician in his own right, Rieu is not the superior of dozens of other less acclaimed waltz violinists around the world. What he and his record label (Universal) have done better than anyone else, however, is to simultaneously allow the bogan to see itself as sophisticated, while pandering to its short attention span, need to be validated, and latent xenophobia. He'll even perform in a suburban mega-mall foodcourt, for those bogans who grow anxious when their pop-classical music consumption becomes separated from their Boost Juice and Krispy Kreme consumption.

Today Tonight

This is the worst show on television. The bogan, with an alarming dependency on it, tunes in each weeknight at 6:30 sharp for its hit of outrage, denial and quick fixes. As the familiar tones of the program's journalistically authoritative host reverberate from the interest-free home theatre system, it lures all occupants of the McMansion into the grand sitting room. Hunched around the television as though it's the only heater in Antarctica, they are ready to receive their 30-minute dosage.

Without this show, the bogan would be lost. It has spent years cultivating a deep hatred of authority, immigrants, young people, non-bogans ripping off bogans, and bogans ripping off bogans. A hatred this huge would topple over under the weight of its own fundamental irrationality unless it was constantly fed and validated by moving pictures and sound. Worse still, if left to its own devices to contemplate its hates, there is a slim but unacceptable possibility that the bogan will realise that it loathes itself.

Thankfully, the bogan can turn to its television at 6:30 pm to ward off any dawning self-awareness. The show's journalists will exercise their own freedom of speech in a bogan-approved manner, cutting off or drowning out anyone featured on the show who attempts to unravel the bogan's fragile social tapestry with an independent opinion. With the boring parts of conventional news reporting eliminated thus, the bogan can immerse itself in the xtreme journalistic elements of ambush, pursuit, hidden cameras and selective editing.

This show is possibly the most finely honed, perfectly evolved bogan-attracting machine in existence. After years of patient trial and error, it has narrowed down the list of stories it presents to eight meta-bogan pieces. It will inform the bogan about:

- how to lose weight without sensible diets or exercise
- the existence of con artists while chasing them down the street
- how generally evil young people are
- the dangers of foreign people entering the country
- what 'crazy stunt' the 'Chaser boys' have recently pulled
- welfare cheats robbing them of their taxes
- any product, service or general notion that will permit the filming of semi-exposed breasts
- any program on the network that might need some extra free advertising.

The bogan will watch this show, then turn on *Home and Away*, and sleep comfortably, content that it is now an empowered and informed member of society. And that nothing is their fault.

A Current Affair

This is the worst show on television. The bogan, with an alarming dependency on it, tunes in each weeknight at 6:30 sharp for its hit of outrage, denial and quick fixes. As the familiar tones of the program's journalistically authoritative host reverberate from the interest-free home theatre system, it lures all occupants of the McMansion into the grand sitting room. Hunched around the television as though it's the only heater in Antarctica, they are ready to receive their 30-minute dosage.

Without this show, the bogan would be lost. It has spent years cultivating a deep hatred of authority, immigrants, young people, non-bogans ripping off bogans, and bogans ripping off bogans. A hatred this huge would topple over under the weight of its own fundamental irrationality unless it was constantly fed and validated by moving pictures and sound. Worse still, if left to its own devices to contemplate its hates, there is a slim but unacceptable possibility that the bogan will realise that it loathes itself.

Thankfully, the bogan can turn to its television at 6:30pm to ward off any dawning self-awareness. The show's journalists will exercise their own freedom of speech in a bogan-approved manner, cutting off or drowning out anyone featured on the show who attempts to unravel the bogan's fragile social tapestry with an independent opinion. With the boring parts of conventional news reporting eliminated thus, the bogan can immerse itself in the xtreme journalistic elements of ambush, pursuit, hidden cameras, and selective editing.

This show is possibly the most finely honed, perfectly evolved bogan-attracting machine in existence. After years of patient trial and error, it has narrowed down the list of stories it presents to eight meta-bogan pieces. It will inform the bogan how to lose weight without fad diets or exercise, inform the bogan about:

- how to lose weight without sensible diets or exercise
- the existence of con artists while chasing them down the street
- how generally evil young people are
- the dangers of foreign people entering the country
- what 'crazy stunt' the 'Chaser boys' have recently pulled
- welfare cheats robbing them of their taxes
- any product, service or general notion that will permit the filming of semi-exposed breasts

- any program on the network that might need some extra free advertising.

 The bogan will watch this show, then turn on *Home and Away*, and sleep comfortably, content that it is now an empowered and informed member of society. And that nothing is their fault.

St Patrick's Day

According to the Australian Bureau of Statistics, only 0.3% of the Australian population was born in Ireland, and only 0.8% are second generation Australians of Irish stock. Seeing as bogans account for at least 20% of the Australian population, it stands to reason that, unless Irish DNA offers a predilection towards being a bogan, there are only around 160,000 Irish bogans. The average age of an Irish immigrant being nearly 50, we at TBL believe that, nationwide, there are only around 20,000–30,000 Irish bogans between 18 and 30 years of age.

 Yet once a year – on 17 March – hundreds of thousands of bogans around the country congregate at Irish pubs and bars and celebrate their Irishness by getting smashed on Guinness and glassing c***s. These bogans will also alter their standard display behaviour. Rather than merely wearing garish t-shirts and posturing aggressively at one another for the benefit of the female, they will wear garish green t-shirts and posture aggressively at one another for the benefit of the female.

 Upon meeting a real Irish person, the bogan will first patronise them by clumsily attempting to put on an Irish accent, and then prepare to fight them, possibly with the ultimate aim of finding gold at the end of the bloodied leprechaun. It's hardly surprising that the bogan has taken to St Patrick's Day with this sort of delusional fervour. After all, the bogan will happily embrace any culture that it perceives to be based on drinking, fighting and people with white skin.

While Irish pubs spend the rest of the year half empty, on St Patrick's Day, the bogan will PAY to enter the same venue and eke out a narrow gap for itself between the toilet door and the cigarette machine. It will then spend the next six hours drinking a beer it shows no interest in for the other 364 days of the year, and complaining about the crowded state of the pub that it never otherwise attends. On its first pint of Guinness, the bogan will inwardly wince at the dense black sludge in its throat, pause to compose itself, and then loudly pronounce its themed deliciousness over the surrounding din. Much of this din is caused by a patently hopeless U2 cover band, earning $500 for a set that is completely devoid of monetary value at any other time.

Indeed, St Patrick's Day is a rare example of the bogan's rampant one-dimensional nationalism being put on the back burner. Today, the bogan will go to great pains to inform bystanders that it is 'one-quarter Irish' (presumably leaving only three-quarters Australian) which, in its mind, qualifies it to enthusiastically recount the same three Irish jokes that it told on St Patrick's Day last year. And the year before. And the year before that.

Two and a Half Men

This show is in no way funny. 'Comedy' is a misnomer in its case. This program is the harbinger of Armageddon. This is the Show Bogans Like. Somewhere, in a dungeon in California, a team of demonic showbiz suits sat down and plotted the destruction of television. *Two and a Half Men* was the result. The combination of

Charlie Sheen – the man who married Denise Richards and entered rehab – teamed with an annoying child and an equally annoying adult, could focus the bogan's self-love by having it assume that Charlie Sheen represents it. The annoying characters presumably play the part of non-bogans in this fantasy.

Offering a heady mix of gratuitous, implied – for PG rating – sex, attractive women and fierce misogyny, the bogan's trigger points are sufficiently charged. This entire show is built up around the cliché that women will reward men for treating them like dirt. Female bogans enjoy this show. The bogan male may try to replicate Charlie Sheen's character's success in real life, but lacking even Sheen's hackneyed wit and addled charm, it will only find positive results at the very, very damaged end of the spectrum.

That this show – riddled with women who are either annoying mothers, obese quasi-lesbians or smoking hot idiots simply begging to fall victim to Charlie Sheen's (read: the bogan's) wiles – is one of the most popular on TV goes to show just how many bogans there are. They could be your friend. They could be your neighbour, your teacher or your accountant. They're out there, watching *Two and a Half Men*.

The presence of a neurotic and ugly but vaguely intelligent character in Charlie's brother provides the perfect impetus for the bogan to feel good about its irrational hatred for intellectuals. It can now comfortably draw an informed conclusion that unless one is sexist, alcoholic, insensitive, and half-successful, they cannot conceivably pull chicks, deftly, like a Pamplona bull hooking a drunken tourist.

There is not even any need for comedy – the evil suits realised that the bogan, pavlovian stereotype that it is, will laugh merely when it is suggested that it is supposed to. Instead of funny or witty dialogue, a deafening laugh track of hyperventilating nitrous oxide victims is thrust into the eardrums of any who dare un-mute their television.

The show's dialogue unrepentantly veers between sexual innuendos, hot chicks and a kid making sexual innuendos, to the rapturous applause of the bogan. The very existence of the 'half-man' (a fine example of the half-baked comedy that plagues the show) joking about menstruation, promiscuity, swearing and other 'adult' issues, makes the bogan terribly excited. How hilarious, it thinks, that a child should not only be aware of such mind-bogglingly complex matters, but also have the ability to turn it into jokes. The show's popularity is further aided by the fact that it is shown on Channel 9. Repeatedly. More times than *Australian Extreme Police Customs Security Force Australia.*

Celebrities' opinions

As has been discussed at length in this convenient hutch of boganic knowledge, the bogan likes to have an opinion. But the process of careful aggregation and analysis of the available data, or long sessions spent staring deep into the inky abstract ether, takes too long in delivering the simple and concrete answers the bogan requires immediately. As a result, the bogan will leave as many stones unturned as possible in seeking out the most convenient shortcut to forming its opinion. The opinions of celebrities are heartily embraced by bogans for this very reason. The bogan believes celebrities embody all that is perfect and unattainable in the temporal realm, so it makes itself a willing vessel for their vacuous musings, which are made readily available to the bogan through the ever-expanding, life-giving tentacles of the malevolent trashmedia.

If there's something that excites a bogan even more than an unqualified celebrity's worthless opinion, it's an unqualified celebrity's worthless opinion on a worthless topic. This is why there were high fives aplenty in the office the day some callous arsehole invented Bert Newton's *20 to One*. A low-balling festival of yawn, this show features unremarkable people discussing banal, pathetic and advertiser-friendly topics such as 'Worst Haircuts', 'Greatest Logies Moments' and 'Hilarious Celebrity Blunders'. Obviously this show is a TV producer's wet dream. Not only does it mainly consist of outtakes and archival footage, but it allows Bert Newton, perennial recipient of an honorary toupee gag at every 'TV Event', to be wheeled out again as an example of just how truly embarrassing this country's entertainment industry is. Celebrity opinion on this rotisserie of shit is provided by a revolving cast of desperate ex-soap stars and reality TV also-rans. And Richard Wilkins.

The bogan, true to form, laps it up like a dog does its own sick. Situated not far from the oft-spatulated base of the TV barrel, somewhere in between *Hey Hey It's Saturday* and TV shows made up of the most popular things on YouTube the previous week, this sort of show used to be served up in the form of once-off outtakes and bloopers specials, whenever there was a hole in a network's programming that needed to be filled as cheaply as possible. The bogan liked these, and wanted more of them. So in the ever-changing, never-amazing world of network TV, where the bogan dollar is king, the bogan can now rely on this torrent of televisual smegma every week.

Clashing with reporters

The bogan knows its rights. It knows that one of those rights is privacy, and that it is particularly entitled to privacy when in public. The bogan is especially protective of its right to privacy when committing criminal acts in public, rioting in public mobs, engaging in episodes of road rage in public, and exiting courthouses in public. The media are nothing but leeches and cockroaches. It is these beliefs that lead the bogan to, when filmed in public against its wishes, clash with reporters. Cameras are smashed, profanities ring through the air, and reporters are assaulted. In many cases, this is recorded by other reporters, causing the bogan to clash with them too.

The bogan does not believe that enforcing its right to privacy in public by clashing with reporters is contradicted by any of its other behaviours. Meanwhile, its appetite for paparazzi shots of celebrities in tabloid magazines remains unquenchable, it continues to audition for *Big Brother* every year (or will when if comes back on air), and reporters are still expected to expose the unsavoury behaviour of other bogans for its infotainment on *Today Tonight* and *A Current Affair*.

There are certain instances in which the bogan will waive its rights to privacy. These include: when waving and gesticulating in the background of live crosses; when not committing a crime or exiting a courthouse; and any other instance in which the bogan deems that the benefits of the publicity to its quest for celebrity status outweigh any negative impact on any ongoing or future civil or criminal proceedings. Most importantly, the bogan will post every minutiae of its existence on Facebook, encouraging the world to view and wonder at the awesomeness of its life. This belief will last until it finds itself clashing with reporters. Suddenly, the bogan will believe that everything it posts online under its own name is entirely private, and not to be viewed by anyone.

The bogan who finds itself clashing with reporters, while rare, will then barricade itself in its home, bemoaning that the papers have the freedom of speech to say things about it, and that the news networks attack it by showing footage of them clashing with reporters. Despite the fact that the bogan is now at least three degrees closer to *Underbelly*, its experience as a notorious person has left it disillusioned and sad.

Cruise ships

When it's not travelling on budget airlines to the exotic countries of Phuket and Bali, the well travelled bogan enjoys sailing the high seas on one of P&O's floating pleasure palaces. The cruise ship represents the epitome of bogan travel, permitting it to chalk up six passport stamps in eight days, visiting foreign countries like Noumea, Port Vila and Suva, without travelling more than 500 metres from a major port and while enjoying all the comforts of home.

Like big things and shopping centres, the bogan is attracted to cruise ships due to their sheer size. A typical ship weighs in at over 70,000 tonnes, has hundreds of rooms, multiple levels and comes equipped with everything a bogan requires: restaurants, nightclubs, casinos, gyms, IMAX theatres and comprehensive in-cabin entertainment. It allows the bogan to eat steak and chips every night, drink stupid quantities of overpriced liquor, gamble, get huge, watch *Avatar* in 3D and enjoy reruns of *Underbelly* from its cabin.

Every day, the cruise ship stops at a different nondescript South Pacific port where the bogan briefly disembarks from its Neptunian chateau to be greeted by some P&O employed, Polynesian-themed dancers. This will prove the closest the bogan will come to a cultural interchange all day, as it spends the next five hours getting bronzed, snorkelling and trying to haggle with more P&O employees at the gift shop for a Pacific themed woodcarving. After a quick coconut cracking demonstration and sarong tying class, the bogan reboards the *Pacific Princess*, feeling for all the world like Captain Cook.

That night, the bogan struggles to peel a prawn from its towering buffet plate, regaling its peers with stories of its near brush with death at the tentacles of a giant killer squid and joking how it saw Lote Tuqiri three times that day. After dinner, it drinks wholesale quantities of Corona and hits the nightclubs, hoping to lure a female bogan back to its cabin where it can feed her this year's designer drug and breach her hull.

DISCRETI⬤NARY SPENDING

No deposit, no interest, no repayments for 18 months!

Maintaining an appropriately fashionable abode, with appropriately massive TV screen and appropriately loud home-theatre system is an expensive task, particularly for the bogan, whose weekly income still relies on night-shift shelf-filling at Woolies. Thankfully, the proprietors of equally massive retailers like Harvey Norman saw a hole in the market, and decided to fill it. So now, bogan dreams can be fulfilled, by getting *free stuff*! That's right, these kindly salespeople will let bogans walk into their store, pick out a 320 cm full HD screen and carry it back to the Holden without paying a cent! Sure, they had to sign a couple of forms before being allowed to leave, but so what? Time to head home and watch *Border Security* in high-definition surround sound!

Of course, none of this takes into account the monthly fees that are mentioned in the fine print of the contract. Nor did the bogan notice the 35% monthly interest that the account accrues immediately upon missing one of these payments, or the cardiac arrest inducing 60% interest that kicks in if the unlucky bogan is still in arrears once the 18 months are up. And it certainly doesn't include burly men arriving at your door at 3 pm, menacingly playing with little Shayleigh and Jaxon, with the tacit implication of kidnap and missing fingers should the withheld funds fail to be procured.

Access to easy credit has been blamed for a lot of things of late, and the bogan's love of free money lies at the heart of all of our economic woes. No job? No assets? No worries! We approve your home loan over the phone! Credit card bill catching up on you? Congratulations, you've just become eligible to double your limit!

Normally, when confronted with thousands of dollars of debt or a looming home repossession, an ordinary person would suck it up and change their spending habits. The bogan, however, is wiser. Cannily placing a call to the producers of *Today Tonight* or *A Current Affair*, it manages to position itself – on national television – as the innocent, only slightly naive victim of malicious predators. The most skilled bogans will even manage to turn the entire episode into a charitable fundraiser, with caring bogans everywhere pledging their financial support. Probably because they, too, remember the sting of Harvey Norman's terms of finance.

Uninformed gambling

The bogan loves to gamble. The thrill of semi-illicit activity is an irresistible call to many, as is the social expectation that men must gamble. However, one visit to the races during a major meet will demonstrate the unambiguous failure of this theory: the bogan doesn't know anything about horse racing. It will wander the lawns at Flemington or Royal Randwick wearing a newly minted pinstripe suit with white crocodile skin shoes and carrying a form guide that it has *no idea how to read*.

It will then proceed to stand in the queue at the bookies, confusedly staring at the mystifying collection of letters and numbers, all the while attempting to look quite the professional punter. Upon arriving at the front of the queue, however, the bogan will invariably place $10 each way on the horse called 'Cunning Stunt' or 'Golden Shower', or some other semi-sexual double entendre.

Then, twenty minutes later, when Far Kennel comes in thirteen lengths behind the winner, it dramatically tears up its ticket, acting for all the world as though some immense equine conspiracy has robbed it of the sure thing that its extensive skills had proffered.

This is the scarcely concealed secret behind the success of gambling industries the world over. What pokies and slots are to septuagenarians, ill-informed sports betting is to the bogan. Billions of dollars are lost to these corporate behemoths as a direct result of male bogan efforts to appear smart and financially successful in front of their female equivalents. This, in turn, is driven by the female bogan's (well, any bogan's for that matter) appreciation of easy money. And there is no easier money than the fabled professional gambler, turning over tens of thousands of dollars on the back of his sophisticated system, in syndication with other veterans of the caper. Instead, they get idiots throwing their money away, only to spend more at the bar drowning their sorrows and bemoaning the horses' inability to get over the line. Even though it was paying $25. And the form guide said it had no chance.

Discount airlines

The bogan is no longer restricted to holidaying within a five-hour Commodore journey of its nest, and it can thank a ginger Englishman for this fact. Now the whole family can whisk itself to the Gold Coast, Sunshine Coast or some other coast with a well-funded regional tourist body that pitches effectively to the bogan's needs. It can even get to 'countries' like Bali, Phuket and other places where there are poor people to haggle with for hair braids. Australia's first discount airline in the modern era was launched in 2000, and Virgin Blue quickly acquired the loyalty of the bogan with its blend of lower prices and titillating hostesses.

Qantas soon realised that the bogan no longer aspired to board the flying Kangaroo, and subsequently launched Jetstar in 2004, with its blend of even lower prices and Magda Szubanski's less persuasive visual charms. To conclude this race to the bottom, Tiger entered the market in 2007, boasting the lowest prices yet, and some scrubbers that the bogan had never heard of. This did not deter the bogan, though, as anyone who has had the misfortune of being situated in a Tiger departure lounge can attest.

The discount airline business model involves stripping airline travel down to the basics, and passing the savings onto the customer. While the bogan generally desires to live like a celebrity, it is very receptive to the idea of getting somewhere really cheaply. This is where the bogan's logic fails on two different levels that it seems unaware of. Firstly, it expects celebrity service at bargain prices. If the discount flight is 30 minutes late, a small cluster of bogans can be seen gesticulating maniacally at the service desk, an act which is likely to make the subsequent flight 45 minutes late. The bogans' flat nasal yowl reverberates across the departure lounge, prompting other bogans to begin howling like a neighbourhood of cross-eyed dogs while the bogan children replenish their tear ducts with 500 ml energy drinks. Due to incidents such as this, the Bali to Brisbane Jetstar flight on Sunday afternoons has come to be known as the 'bogan bus'.

Secondly, the bogan has saved *twenty-seven dollars* on a flight from Melbourne to Sydney at dinner time this Saturday, flying Tiger instead of Qantas at 9 am on Wednesday. Let's break it down, shall we?

	Tiger	Qantas
Ticket cost	$78	$105
TWENTY-SEVEN DOLLAR SAVING!!!		
15 kg of luggage	$10	$0
Credit card fee	$6	$7.70
Snack on flight	$5	$0
Two beers on flight	$12	$0
Dollar value of time wasted after check-in	$15 (45 mins)	$10 (30 mins)
SUBTOTAL	**$126**	**$122.70**
Plus Dignity cost of bogans in Tiger terminal	$100	$0
GRAND TOTAL	**$226**	**$122.70**

Chrisco hampers

'After months of excited waiting, it's finally arrived. OMG. A massive hamper full of festive goodness from Chrisco! Sure, it's a couple of weeks later than they said it'd be but, kids, come quickly – our magical Christmas is saved!'

This has been the triumphal squawk emanating from bogan nests around Australia as, one by one, they receive their big baskets of goodies. After years of piously soothing advertisements from a middle-aged woman with a vague resemblance to Mrs Claus, bogan families have fallen for Chrisco en masse. With festive food hampers ranging from $370 to a galling $1250, this clever company has somehow convinced bogans that waiting to have a massive basket of easily available foodstuffs sent to them is better than immediately getting the actual items they want from the supermarket up the road at half the price.

The key to the appeal of Chrisco is the idea of making direct debit instalments all year in order to have the hamper arrive for FREE sometime in December. Clearly, this is a gift from the good people at Chrisco, massive earlier investment notwithstanding. As the bogan appears willing to invest $210 over nine months in order to have a slab of Bundy and Coke appear magically on its doorstep, Chrisco appears willing to make enormous profits from their gullibility.

As the bogan 'plans its finances' in advance, it allows Chrisco to sit on a lucrative mountain of bogan bucks for months before it has to actually purchase inventory for the hampers sometime in October. In order to deal with pesky questions about value, Chrisco sincerely informs the bogan about the stresses and strains that abound when navigating the supermarket in December, as though there's some kind of bogan demilitarised zone between the dairy aisle and the turkey fridge. Instead, it's okay. Chrisco is here to help. Thank heavens for Chrisco.

The Chrisco company originally formed in the UK, where it was moderately successful. While Britain is riddled with boganesque Chavs, the founders recognised that, with its apparently far more limited grasp of accounting, the bogan populace in the antipodes could make them rich beyond their wildest imaginings. They moved to New Zealand, and from there the company crossed the Tasman to storm the main bogan stronghold in 1997. Today, it fleeces over a million bogans per year, and turns over a cool quarter billion. This phenomenal cash harvesting often goes unnoticed, as Chrisco is a seasonal business without prominent shopfronts, and bogans rarely read anything with numbers.

In late 2007, a systems crash caused the company to fail to deliver thousands of hampers prior to Christmas, which made the bogans both furious and elated. Furious, because they had to go to the supermarket to chance their luck at Checkpoint Charlie. Elated, because it allowed them to conduct furious vox pops with 22-year-old *Today Tonight* reporters about a new, and enormous, rort. However, while bogan rage is intense, a crippled attention span causes it to also be brief. A month later, the bogans in question had already signed up for an extortionate 43-week instalment plan for Christmas 2008. This is the distillation of everything that bogans love about buying things.

Like some kind of retarded Friedmanite, the bogan views Chrisco as a good deal. This is the bogan economy. In the belief that if something is paid for in instalments, and purchased in bulk, it must be sensible commerce, the bogan parts with $4.70 a week. For ten months. To get a slab of Bundy and Cokes and a towel.

As presented on their website, though, the hampers appear full to the brim with discounted factory seconds. This mass of consumerism tends to cause an eye twitch in many of us, however, and we can find the ludicrous price/image conflation confusing. But it's okay, TBL is here to help. Here is a breakdown of a couple of the simplest beverage hampers on offer:

Coca-Cola hamper Contains two slabs of coke (supermarket value $35), and a promotional beach towel, hat, Frisbee and bag. Typically this stuff is only a few bucks each (or free) when Coke puts a promotion on, because basically it's advertising.

Chrisco price: $137.80, or *only $3.21 per week!* Only $3 a week for all that Cokey Christmasy goodness? Thanks for the 300% markup, Chrisco – Christmas will be magical!

Beers of the world hamper Contains six 6-packs of mid-priced beer (supermarket value $15 each, total $90), and a 5 litre mini keg of Heineken (supermarket value $30).

Chrisco price: $202.80, or *only $4.73 per week!* Only $4 a week for all that beery Christmasy goodness? Thanks, Chrisco, for only charging $80 for delivery. Christmas will be magical!

This is the most genius company in Australia. And bogans bend over and take it with a smile.

Post Xmas sales

The weeks leading up to Christmas are expensive but pleasurable for the bogan. Many bogans get drawn into the endless loop of trying to outdo their other relatives in terms of the scale, shininess, or brand naminess of their gifts. This, predictably enough, is funded by interest-free credit card debt at a competitive 20% interest per annum. Christmas Day comes, the gifts are exchanged, the sugary parts of the Chrisco hamper are consumed, and bogans nationwide retire to their beds on the evening of the 25th, exhausted, broke, but content.

This period of contentment lasts from 11 pm on 25 December until approximately 3 am on December 26, when the bogan female pounces out of bed, a glimmer in her eye. Shopping time. The Boxing Day sales at department stores are due to start in as little as two hours hence, and it is of vital importance to the bogan female that it heads the waiting throng. Once upon a time, Boxing Day was associated with hosting alternate family gatherings, relaxing at the park with friends and loved ones, or getting kicked out of bay 13 at the cricket. Today, however, it is entirely and resolutely tied in with spending immense amounts of money for products no one needs at surprisingly negligible discounts.

The clock ticks past 6 am. The lights are on in the store, there are employees milling around in there, but the doors remain closed. The bogans are growing increasingly agitated, united in their outrage at having their consumption delayed by tens of seconds. At 6:02, two security guards approach the doors from inside, and begin instructing the bogan mob in how to gracefully enter the shopping centre.

Without warning, a particularly ox-like bogan female barrels at the door, and the security guards soon relent. The bogans surge, foaming at the mouth and desperately snatching at any item within a two-metre radius of a sign saying '(up to) 70% OFF!' Skinny bogans wriggle their way between the fat ones, tall ones reach over the top, and the fat ones jut their ample rumps outwards to create a quivering exclusion zone around the precious discounts.

On Boxing Day, the gladiatorial bogan is able to fight to impulse purchase items it does not want, at prices that are cheaper than what it won't pay. It justifies this on the basis of being broke from Christmas, necessitating frugality, and any discount is, by virtue of its discounted nature, a saving. While all of the things it set out to purchase are either not on sale or already gone, the bogan is determined not to leave this feeding frenzy empty handed.

At 8:45 am, the bogan limps out of David Jones sporting a black eye, a torn t-shirt and a David Jones bag containing an electric mango slicer, a half-price Christmas tree, and a set of carving knives by a company it has never heard of and cannot pronounce. And only $220 poorer.

X factor

Etymology and leXicography are fascinating subjects, dedicated to understanding how language develops as it does, while offering fascinating insight into the way we speak and write today. Despite centuries of study, however, eminent linguists are at a loss to Xplain one thing: why bogans will pay for anything with the letter X in it.

Like backpackers to a sperm bank, bogans began to gravitate towards any product with a large (often colourful) 'X' on the packaging. The trend was slow in forming. The bogan, with its love of tXt-friendly abbreviations – well before tXting Xisted – embraced Xmas, possibly the first step in this process. A basic, secular way of taking Jesus out of Jesus' birthday, Xmas spoke to the bogan need for simplicity, even as they spent a great deal of time decrying the political correctness gone mad of a fictional nativity scene at a fictional school being cancelled in order to avoid offending local terrorists.

Around the same time, bogan forebears fell in love with INXS, a band whose simple, personalised numberplate-ready moniker suggested that despite their stunning international success, they simply arrived before their time. Soon, quick-thinking marketing types were thumping every product they had with a massive X. The X was closely linked to Xtremeness, and despite the fact that these products were often Xtremely shit, Xtremely Xpensive and Xtremely unnecessary, bogans adopted them in droves.

When Pepsi wanted to sell diet Pepsi to bogan males, it labelled it Pepsi MAX. Porn wasn't proper porn unless it was XXX. Simon Cowell realised that *Pop Idol* was shit, so made it again and called it *X-Factor*, and conquered the UK. Functional water absolutely had to have a variety called XXX. Hollywood Xecutives also moved in. They created the *X-Files* to fan the flames of bogan conspiracy theories. They then skipped a whole bunch of steps in the creative process – including plot, character and script – and did two things: hired Vin Diesel and made a film called *XXX*, secure in the knowledge that bogans would flock to see a film with that many Xs. That the film contained zero faux-lesbianism (this X, being silent, is incidentally confusing to the bogan) was only ameliorated by a scene involving Diesel snowboarding faster than an avalanche, just like they would expect to see in the X-games.

Bogans soon began inserting the letter X into names that it had no place being in in the first place, pumping out Jaxon after Saxon. The bogan has yet to discover the XX, although it can't be long now. Also, after creating so many new Xisting new generation bogans, the older bogan – some from generation X – often realises that there is one X it can't stand. Its X-husband. Or the X-chromosome.

SMS-speak

In da earli dayz of digital mobile telephony, it wuz devised dat lil chunks of data could b regularly transmitted az test signals from phones 2 towers 2 rfrsh info. An example of this is da 'cell info display' fnctn, which tells u what town or suburb ur in @ ne givn time. Cuz these test signals only get fired thru wen there's spare capacity in da ntwrk, they effectively cre8 no xtra demand or bottlenex.

LOL, OMG, WTF, BRB, IMHO, SUM1, SXE.

It wuz also realised in da 90s dat dere might b a commercial application 4 this test signal, in da form of text msgs btwn users. There wuz an engineering limit of 160 characters in da signal, so dat became da size of a text msg. As it turns out, da bogan is deeply in <3 wit the SMS. Bcuz da bogan rarely has neting subtle or nuanced 2 say, 160 characters is almost always enuf, unless da bogan in question is a 16-yr-old girl who enters her illegible stream of consciousness in2 her keypad for mins @ a time.

2MRW, GTG, PMSL, L8R, GR8, TTYL, WKND.

Da othr big ting dat bogans hav gained frm SMS is SMS-speak. Tired of bein told dat it cant spell, the bogan has cr8ed an elabor8 system of space saving remixd xtreme words, dat allow it 2 fit more inane babble in2 160 characters. Bcuz all of da words r wrong, da bogan cn project its aptitude for pl@itude as '@itude'. These communiqués cre8 a time-consuming and frustr8ing decryption task 4 ne unfortun8 non-bogan recipients.

AFAIK, NE1, PLZ, ROFL, LMAO, 2NITE.

In da same way dat a bogan is prone 2 updating its fb status many times per day 2 broadcast da minutiae of its existence, it can bcome hopelessly hooked on SMS. Many bogans will pump out thousands of msgs per month, wit a total amount of substance comparable 2 a piece of navel lint. Globally, 4.1 trillion SMS msgs were sent in 08, billions of these by and 2 bogans. Da phone companies, meanwhile, harvest hundreds of millions of $z from this compulsion. As mentioned earlier, da telcos need 2 invest in 0 additional infrastructure 2 earn mountains of bogan SMS $z. It's basically a financial colostomy bag, linking da bogan's phone & wallet pockets, & transmitting da $z back 2 HQ in a packet of test data of 160 digits or less.

ThEn, ThErE r PrEmIuM SMS SeRvIcEs. OMFG.

English translation for the non-bogan In the early days of digital mobile telephony, it was devised that small chunks of data could be regularly transmitted as test signals from phones to towers to refresh information. An example of this is the 'cell info display' function, which tells you what town or suburb you're in at any given time. Because these test signals only get fired through when there's spare capacity in the network, they effectively create no extra demand or bottlenecks.

Laugh out loud, oh my god, what the fuck, be right back, in my humble opinon, someone, sexy.

It was also realised in the 1990s that there might be a commercial application for this test signal, in the form of text messages between users. There was an engineering limit of 160 characters in the signal, so that became the size of a text message. As it turns out, the bogan is deeply in love with SMS. Because the bogan rarely has anything subtle or nuanced to say, 160 characters is almost always enough, unless the bogan in question is a 16-year-old girl who enters her illegible stream of consciousness into her keypad for minutes at a time.

Tomorrow, got to go, pissing myself laughing, later, great, talk to you later, weekend.

The other big thing that bogans have gained from SMS is SMS-speak. Tired of being told that it can't spell, the bogan has created an elaborate system of space saving remixed xtreme words that allow it to fit more inane babble into 160 characters. Because all of the words are wrong, the bogan can project its aptitude for platitude as 'attitude'. These communiqués create a time-consuming and frustrating decryption task for any unfortunate non-bogan recipients.

As far as I know, anyone, please, rolling on the floor laughing, laughing my arse off, tonight.

In the same way that a bogan is prone to updating its Facebook status many times per day to broadcast the minutiae of its existence, it can become hopelessly hooked on SMS. Many bogans will pump out thousands of messages per month, with a total amount of substance comparable to a piece of navel lint. Globally, 4.1 trillion SMS messages were sent in 2008, billions of these by and to bogans. The phone companies, meanwhile, harvest hundreds of millions of dollars from this compulsion. As mentioned earlier, the telcos need to invest in zero additional infrastructure to earn mountains of bogan SMS bucks. It's basically a financial colostomy bag, linking the bogan's phone and wallet pockets, and transmitting the dollars back to HQ in a packet of test data of 160 digits or less.

Then, there are premium SMS services. Oh my fucking god.

Tiffany & Co.

The female bogan will tell you that it likes Tiffany & Co. jewellery. It is lying to you. In an elaborate and costly attempt to conceal this lie, it will spend many hundreds of dollars on Tiffany products. In a final act of masochism, the bogan will clench its teeth and wear its Tiffany jewellery every day. So why does the bogan cause itself this much pain? Let's investigate.

In November 2009, Tiffany & Co. opened a new retail store at Melbourne's upmarket bogan-magnet, Chadstone shopping complex. The bogan is always tempted to go to these high-profile events. Maybe there would be classy celebrities there, like Bec Hewitt. The femme-bogue has followed the Hewitts' storybook romance via the trashmedia Kraken, and one of the most beautiful and touching parts was when Lleyton gave Bec a $200,000 Tiffany's engagement ring. The female bogan's admiration for fine couture and luxury goods is well known, and Chadstone has all the *Sex and the City*-approved stores, including Louis Vuitton, Gucci and Jimmy Choo. What's also well known is the bogan's ability to fight through the throngs and storm the doors.

Well, usually. This time, the femme-bogue sees something that stops it in its tracks. There is a line outside the Tiffany doors, and not any just any ordinary line. A line with a velvet rope. The bogan joins the line and excitedly awaits the treasures within the store. After waiting for what seems like hours and sending about 7000 text messages, the bogan is nodded through the doors by an exquisitely suited man. Having to wait in a classy and exclusive line generally only happens outside of a nightclub, and the bogan feels itself tipping into spending overdrive. Its credit card quivers in fear.

Inside, the bogan examines the shiny, expensive things. The problem for the bogan is that most of them don't really look the way they should. The pieces are too subtle, too classic. The femme-bogue's initial elation at entering such a classy place has turned to rage. Why spend $5500 on a square linked white gold necklace, if someone five metres away can't clearly see how classy it is? The bogan's craving for public recognition of its luxury status must be fed.

When the bogan is leaving the store, it is conspicuously swinging a blue Tiffany & Co. shopping bag. After selecting an extra large bracelet with a heart shaped silver tag on it, saying: 'Please Return to Tiffany & Co. New York'. Now everyone will know how tasteful the bogan is.

Of course, as with all luxury goods, the bogan only wants more. And the femme-bogue loves buying jewellery so much, it even buys miniature jewellery to form into wearable metajewellery. On its next visit to the store, the bogan is likely to see the Tiffany &

Co. shopping bag charm, with enamel finish in sterling silver. For just $285, the bogan will be able to wear as jewellery, a homage to shopping for jewellery. This will create a semantic vortex from which it will never emerge.

The third dimension

Avatar has made $2.7 billion at the global box office. It stands to reason that at least $2.65 billion of that has come directly from bogans' fraying surf-branded wallets. While there is no doubt that the film's pretence of taking care of primitive natives by not blowing them up allows the bogan to feel cosmopolitan, what it finds really appealing is massive blue alien side boob. Side boob that can now be seen IN 3D! Moreover, Corey Worthington's brother Jake Sully was busily saving the natives on the bogans' behalf IN 3D! A one dimensional actor IN 3D!

3D! has revolutionised the film industry, just as it has revolutionised the amount the bogan is willing to pay for its plasma screen IN 3D! While the bogan knows it likes its massive cans in DD, adding a third D creates THE THIRD DIMENSION! IN 3D! The bogan can now pay more to watch the same film, but emerge dazed and with a niggling, persistent headache that will take a number of hours to fully resolve IN 3D!

The plasma screen with built-in 3D! allows the manufacturer to charge the bogan a metric underbelly-gutload of extra cash for a TV that then lets the bogan run the risk of causing maxtreme epilepsy – which, to the bogan, is the ultimate spurious allergy IN 3D! Samsung is the first company to retail 3D! televisions in Australia, and the $1000+ price premium means that the bogan will require a 3D! credit card debt to own its max intense home theatre experience. Samsung has also offered the bogan the chance to power up its face, in preparation for the maxtreme dimensional onslaught that watching *Under, Over and Around Belly* in 3D! will provide, by wearing 3D! glasses with a power button IN 3D!

Yes, you heard right, *Underbelly* will come in 3D! in 2011. The bogan has long felt a deep personal affiliation with *Underbelly*, and in 2011 it will finally be immersed in a maelstrom of boobs, bullets and bodybags IN 3D! This new level of intimacy will prompt the bogan to refer to *Underbelly* characters by their first names, and any bogan who has done a short course in photography will be in hot demand to photograph other bogans in the midst of the cast IN 3D! With this newly rabid desire to max out the dimensions it exists in, the Nine Network is also paying $10,000,000 to bring out an American camera crew to film the NRL State of Origin game IN 3D! This will be the first time the bogan can tell other bogans to fuck off because its state is full IN 3D! It is understood that Max Markson is currently exploring the legal ramifications of engineering a sex scandal perpetrated by a dimension.

Cross promotions

Despite its serene and benevolent exterior, the bogan is a seething pit of hatred. It despises the task of fact checking, it reviles independent information sources. And it is downright disgusted by any smartarse who claims to have figured out anything that the bogan has not. As a result, the bogan is fertile ground for an elaborate web of corporate cross-promoting that it remains entirely oblivious to. This pleaseth the marketer.

The bogan elects to snuggle itself entirely within the willing arms of three commercial TV stations, one News Limited online portal, and one News Limited print newspaper. Never leaving the advertising matrix for a moment, the bogan develops a self-concept that is inextricably linked to the products that are pitched at its age, gender, and aspirational segment. The bogan's ego skyrockets when it purchases what it is told to, but when it purchases a product with more than one branding, the maths enters the realm of quantum boganics. A cross-promotion between any two things that the bogan likes is enormously soothing to the bogan, offering it a synchronised and seamless way to dispose of all of its available dollars and hours, along with some that shouldn't be available at all.

The marketer's ability to install new things that bogans like via cross promotion is about the best way to overcome the bogan's distrust of change. Got a car racing format that is struggling in a crowded marketplace? Get P!nk to gyrate in a TV ad for it. Trying to endear a turgid new R'n'B chanteuse to the bogan market? Promote it on *Video Hits* by offering a prize of a max obnoxious stereo system from Sony that the bogan already wants.

All of this purchasing of related items is likely to make the bogan hungry, and when it marches its brood down to McDonald's, the bogan's children demand a Happy Meal, which is subsidised by the Disney corporation via whatever Pixar is peddling these school holidays. Figurine in hand, the child demands to see the movie, the celeb scoop for which the bogan saw on the *Today* show the previous week. Orange plasticine puppet Richard Wilkins also told the bogan about the latest *Underbelly* cast exclusive in *Woman's Day* magazine, which features shock snaps of a Nine Network personality eating McDonald's with a new lover. All of this frenetic gossip-discovering has made the bogan hungry.

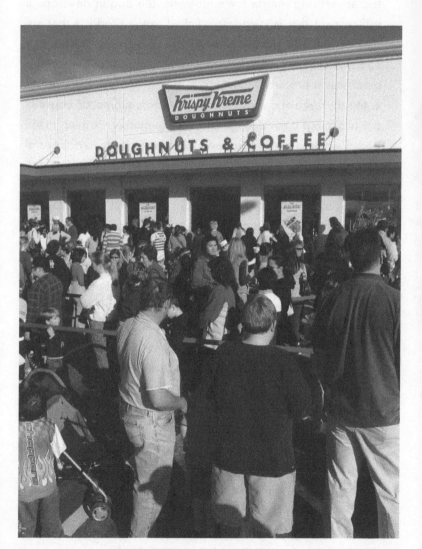

GASTRON●MY

Massive cans

Ever since energy drinks caught the bogan's eye at about the turn of the century, the Coca-Cola company has wanted in. Brands like Red Bull and V had figured out how to reduce the can size by a third, put more caffeine in, and charge twice as much. This is commonly referred to as 'marketing genius'. Due to their uncharacteristically poor understanding of the Things Bogans Like, Coca-Cola's attempt to gain traction in this lucrative area failed again and again. First came 'Lift Plus' in 2000, which was a spin-off of an established brand, put into a slim can. This didn't sell well, so they decided to do the exact same thing a couple of years later, but call it 'Sprite Recharge'. Unsurprisingly, the bogan remained unmoved. The company then launched 'Burn' in 2003, a slim 250 ml beverage with minimal xtremeness. Fail.

In 2007, evidence emerged that Coca-Cola's inept marketing department was getting closer to understanding the bogan. Accompanied by a $15 million advertising campaign, they launched 'Mother'. The can was covered in tribal tattoos, had an aggressive font, and the name of the product allowed the bogan to make endless jokes such as 'I've got your mother in my mouth LOL'. Despite these improving lures, the bogan did not like the taste, and there was still something missing. It failed.

The next product launch worked, even though they only repackaged the Mother brand. Why? They reverted the taste to one of their previous unsuccessful attempts, and kept the tattooed aggressive can design. They slightly upped the obnoxiousness of the rhetoric, including phrases such as 'our lame legal guys made us warn you', which appeals to the bogan's desire to feel like it can and does break all the rules. But this paled into insignificance in comparison with the true reason the bogan suddenly embraced Mother. Coke doubled the size of the can to a hulking 500 ml. At the end of the day, all the bogan wants is the widest TV, the loudest clothes, the fastest jet ski and the biggest biceps. The bogan love of maxtremity means that the quality of a product and what it does mean nothing compared to whether it is either (a) bigger than its neighbours or (b) provides the bogan equivalent of value for money.

Coca-Cola could then rest easy, knowing that there were thousands of bogans walking the streets fingering an oversized mother. Indeed, it has been so successful that both V and Red Bull have launched larger cans to defend their market share. Speaking of massive cans, bogans love enormous breasts, too.

Mexican beer

We've already dealt with the fact that the bogan enjoys beers that are brewed here but labelled as foreign to give the fictional imprimatur of international cool. The bogan, however, is entirely, blissfully unaware that the repackaged Crown Lager it is drinking is Australian made. Thus, it has no real need to be discerning when it comes to alcohol, beyond that fact that the beer must be from another country. This conveniently explains why the only genuinely foreign beer the bogan drinks tastes like cat's piss, and requires citrus-based assistance to enter the nebulous realm of 'drinkable'.

Mexicans cannot give their entry level beer away fast enough in their native land. Having realised some time ago that bogans are stupid, however, they began exporting their swill to Australia at premium prices. At velvet-roped leisure venues around Australia,

Corona can sell for as much as $9 a bottle. Back home in Mexico, the same product will sell for $14 per case, or under $2 each at a licensed venue. Drinking a pale, watery version of beer somehow confers cultural cachet onto the bogan, purely because it is sourced from a Latin American country with many poor people.

When the bogan orders a Corona or Sol, the bartender simply assumes that it would require a slice of lime. Originally, the bogan inserted a slice of lemon into their colourless liquor, but it rapidly became clear that this only made the beer taste worse. The presence of citrus itself has been hugely successful in attracting the female bogan to beer, a task previously thought to be beyond the capacity of mortal man. By placing a tart piece of fruit on the rim of the bottle, the drink now attains the appearance, and hence the status, of a cocktail. Mexican beer is cool.

The Mexican beer the bogan is drinking also matches the t-shirt the bogan is wearing, which has a Mexican location and a date on it which strangely links the bogan to the shooting of Emiliano Zapata. The bogan is unaware of the significance of the numbers and letters on its shirt, but any shame in this is unrelated to it tearing off its shirt after 15 Mexican beers, and commencing a glassing joust on the footpath outside.

Manly diet cola

The female bogan has long been very interested in not being fat, and engaged in various fad diets, fleeting exercise regimens and superstitions, with the hope of attaining the physique of whichever starlet Richard Wilkins was polluting that week. The male bogan, meanwhile, was ten blocks up the road, wolfing down beer and KFC at Shano's house.

So too was there a gulf between how the male and female bogan felt about diet cola. The female bogan embraced it with gusto from the outset, glad to have an image conscious method of carbo offsetting the nutritional villainy of fast food. The male bogan staunchly resisted all attempts to get it to drink diet cola. The idea of being on a diet made it feel faulty, disempowered, and feminine. All of these feelings were horrific beyond words to the alpha bogan, which prided itself on being manly and tough to the max.

Thankfully, Pepsi had an ear to the ground during the male bogan's existential crisis. In December 1994, it gave the male a chance to be on a secret diet while propping up its paper-thin self-esteem . . . to the MAX. The packaging was xtreme, the can was black instead of wimpy girly white/silver, and the font was aggressive. All of the elements were in place for the emerging product category of 'maxtreme male diet cola'. Pepsi Max even sponsored the fastest rollercoaster in the world, to prove beyond doubt that the drink was super xtreme. They failed to mention to the bogan that it did not differ in any meaningful way from Diet Pepsi, and the male bogan was glad not to hear it.

After a decade of gradual progress, Pepsi Max was doing well. Coca-Cola looked across and remarked, 'We too must make our cola maxtreme for the bogan'. In early 2006, Coca-Cola Australia launched a disastrously naive internet viral campaign called 'The Zero Movement' which it hoped would convince young people via street posters, websites, manifestos, and stupid impractical slogans that they should become more xtreme. Their biggest failure since not making Mother xtreme for the bogan, the campaign was soon canned. They then got back to marketing the product itself, rather than some idiotic notion of underground revolution, and it did quite well to emerge from Pepsi Max's slipstream. Coke Zero also had the black label, robust font and notion of manliness that the male bogan craves in its secret diets, and the word 'Zero' even contains the second most bogan-cherished letter in the alphabet.

This challenge from Coca-Cola made Pepsi step up in 2010. Bus stop billboards around the country are carrying their black poster announcing 'HEY SUGAR, YOU'RE FIRED!' in jagged capital letters. It helps the bogan male to feel as though its can of Pepsi Max allows it to totally dominate its world to the xtreme. It even comes with just a sprinkling of old school gender misogyny that allows the male bogan to feel in charge of the bitch that is the sucrose labour force as it sips on its pissy diet cola.

Sushi

The bogan is xtremely wary of all things foreign. Refugees taking its job. Terrorists blowing up its local Westfield mega-mall. Foreign investors buying its McMansions. Asian people secretly putting cats and whales in its beef and black bean. But, beacon of culture and tolerance that the bogan is, it has allowed a select few pieces of international cuisine to penetrate its foreign food forcefield.

One such dish is sushi. For years, the bogan feared – or simply did not know about – sushi. Sushi bars and other Asian style eateries were popping up in the bogan's local shopping centre foodcourt, but their exotic origins made the bogan uncomfortable and provided proof of the 'Asian invasion' it had heard about from reputable tabloid television sources. The bogan avoided these places in a show of national solidarity, continuing its vast consumption of McDonald's and KFC.

But that all changed following a meeting between powerful Japanese executives, high up in a Tokyo skyscraper, which sought to address poor sushi sales in Australia. After much bowing and brow furrowing, it was realised that only hipsters and Japanese tourists were eating sushi in Australia. They had completely missed the big spending, big eating, xenophobic but marketing-malleable mass-market known as the bogan. But how to sell strange foreign food to this tightly packed herd of plain-palated conformists? Then one particularly cynical marketing genius suggested, 'What if we sell the California roll in Australia, and replace the wasabi with a mild, flavourless paste, but still call it wasabi?'

The California roll had been invented by sushi chefs in California in the 1970s to make the dish more palatable for Americans, and the only strategy more effective than creating an equivalent Australianised dish was to retain the link to America, where everything is bigger and, therefore, better. Because California is where celebrities are, the association is taken by the bogan to be a celebrity endorsement. And the 'wasabi' provides an avenue for the bogan to demonstrate its hardness while simultaneously allowing it to wax nostalgic about former *Australian Idol* contestant Lee Harding's song of the same name.

Wine tours

The bogan does not like wine. Wine does not come in a ready-to- drink can, it does not require the addition of fruit, grape varieties have foreign sounding names, and wine glasses are terrible for glassing folk. Unless the bogan has ascended to Carey-esque heights of boganity. There is, however, one exception to this rule . . . wine tours. On a wine tour, the bogan is instantly transformed into a knowledgeable and enthusiastic wine buff, a connoisseur of all things viticultural, a regular James Halliday.

The tour starts early, departing from a shopping centre carpark at 8:00 am, and restricted to any of the six wineries in Australia that the bogan has previously heard of. Hungover and cranky from the night before (despite explicit instructions to stay off the grog for a night), the busload of bogans stop at Macca's for a sausage-and-egg McMuffin to line their respective stomachs for the day ahead. Three Beam and colas/vodka cruisers and a few choruses from 'Sex on Fire' later, the group arrives at the first winery.

After a quick tour of the winery itself – in which they rapidly become bored and start asking 'When do we get to drink wine?' – the restless horde of bogans descend on the tasting room like one-legged seagulls on a burnt chip. Greedily scanning the tasting notes, the males in the group immediately demand to taste the winery's reserve $100 2001 shiraz (the one with 'NOT FOR TASTING' written after it), while the females ask the exasperated winemaker if he makes any Marlborough sav blanc.

Angrily settling for wines actually available to taste, the male bogans then try to outdo each other, carefully examining their glasses, sticking their noses ineffectually into their glass and repeatedly swirling their wine until most of it ends up on their designer singlets, they search their limited lexicons for adjectives in which to describe the wine. Having managed to come up with a few words ranging from 'fruity' to 'white' and 'red', the bogan sneaks a glance at the back of the bottle before loudly commenting on its 'young body', 'minerally nose' and 'hint of cinnamon'.

While this argument takes place, the female bogans chuckle conspiratorially with each other as they speak of how awful chardonnay is, in the belief that this confers the requisite level of wine snobbery onto them. This continues until the sommelier points out that the last three glasses they each gleefully put away were the winery's three most recent vintages of chardonnay.

After sampling the winery's entire range twice, the bogan refuses to purchase any wine. When politely told he's had enough, the bogan becomes angry and unsuccessfully tries to glass the sales staff. The bogan is not adept at brandishing a fluted glass in anger, preferring the predictable squatness of the pint.

Remembering that he thinks wine is shit anyway, the bogan retreats to the safety of the bus and the more familiar taste of premixed drinks and the soothing tones of Caleb Followill.

Krispy Kreme

While the bogan has used doughnuts to medicate its desire for fat and sugar many times in the past, these were just ordinary doughnuts. Now a whole new world of bogan-style doughtnuts has opened up. Dispensing with flavour in favour of koncentrated sugar and fat, in mid-2003 the American kompany opened its first Australian store in Sydney. Not available anywhere else, rumour of Krispy Kreme's ability to attach sugar to the *side* of the doughnut ran wild in bogan circles. Soon, Jetstar was ferrying thousands of karry-on doughnuts per week, as intrepid bogan ants scuttled their exotic treats back to nests around Australia. After a period of establishing brand mythology in the bogan psyche, Krispy Kreme was ready for phase two.

On Thursday, 2 March 2006 at the QV retail komplex in central Melbourne a queue hundreds of bogans long is snaking its way up and down the walkways of the komplex, erratically doubling back on itself in open spaces wide enough to allow the bogans to do so. A Krispy Kreme doughnut giveaway promotion is running in the building, and the bogan is queuing for up to three hours in the hope of getting one of the 10,000 free doughnuts on offer. There is no velvet rope in sight, but the bogan is desperate.

Three hours in a queue for the possibility of a free $3 doughnut. Few kompanies have been more successful in manipulating boganomics to their own ends. As each bogan proudly marched away from the kounter bearing its doughnut, Krispy Kreme knew that it was the start of a beautiful relationship. While the American parent kompany has been trading very poorly in recent years, the Australian bogan has almost single-handedly kept the operation afloat. Kanada's 18 stores have dwindled to three, Hong Kong's seven stores went into liquidation in 2008, and store numbers in the United States halved between 2004 and 2009. But the bogan remained as firm as a doughnut-filled gut kan remain. There are now 54 stores in Australia, and rising.

Why does the bogan like Krispy Kreme so much? Well, apart from the bogan-titillating branding and launch kampaign, the kompany has also made life very easy for the bogan. What other kompany is kind enough to offer a 24-hour doughnut and watery koffee drive-through at Fountain Gate in Melbourne, and Penrith in Sydney? After the launch of the Fountain Gate store, there was a bogan kar queue 500 metres long which had to be soothed by local police and security guards to avoid doughnut-related glassings. But while a network of 54 franchised stores offered reasonable bogan koverage, there was more to do. Krispy Kreme successfully negotiated to get its premium priced doughnuts stocked at Woolworths, and at selected petrol stations.

Now the bogan would never be denied its konstitutional right to spend $25 on a dozen shiny 25% fat doughnuts from a kar-friendly outlet near to its McMansion.

Meat Lovers' Pizza

The occasional bogan wants to become vegetarian. Really. However, in a rare example of self-awareness, it knows it has no control over its pathological need for protein, which as far as the bogan knows exists only in beef, chicken and Max Bulk Powder 4000. Therefore, the only logical response to the bogan's desire to be herbivorous is to first eat *all* of the animals. This is more difficult than it sounds. There are many animals, and the bogan's appetite for destruction is limited to eighties hair metal and an aversion to salad.

While the bogan is uncomfortable with the idea of where the protein injection comes from, and would most likely shirk at the idea of skinning a cow (despite its boisterous statements), it is perfectly comfortable with consuming the fruits of others' labour. Male bogans are on an ongoing dietary mission to depopulate entire species via any and all means necessary. Not content with catastrophically disrupting marine environments with fishing boats and jet skis, the bogan has looked further abroad.

Pizza Hut saw this and responded. The male bogan has a clear predisposition to label all green foods as for poofs, and continually derides salads as 'rabbit feed' or 'chicks' food'. Pizza Hut realised that while the bogan was already partial to a large margarita, that particular variety, in its effort to avoid giving nutritional offence, had avoided almost every food the bogan genuinely pursues. So they visited the slaughterhouse and said, 'I'll take it.'

Thus the bogan was gifted with the Meat Lovers' Pizza. It is the quarter-pounder of mock Italian food, Hemingway on a yeasty base, an atomic protein overdose. Covered in sufficient barbecue sauce to drown an actual cow, the pizza then successfully removes all meat flavour, which is fortuitous as it would possibly turn the bogan to vegetarianism, a previously inconceivable event. When the bogan has the option of 75 different varieties of processed meat slathered in cheese, meat, tomato, meat and meat, all other dining options fade into an amorphous green mass.

Last year, there were about 170,000 hospitalisations nationwide for coronary heart disease, and it is TBL's understanding that the Meat Lovers' Pizza is responsible for at least 450,000,000,000 of them. Faced with the choice between the Supreme, the Hawaiian (bogans, in a rare display of taste, decry the application of pineapple to pizza), the Capricciosa or the Meat Lovers', the bogan will invariably gravitate to the meal most likely to induce a fatal disease. Not fearful of cardiac arrest but concerned about an expansion of waist or thigh, the bogan makes up for this colossal intake of saturated fats with a SureSlim shake, a manly diet coke and a few sessions on the AbMaster7400, then hits the sack, healthy and happy.

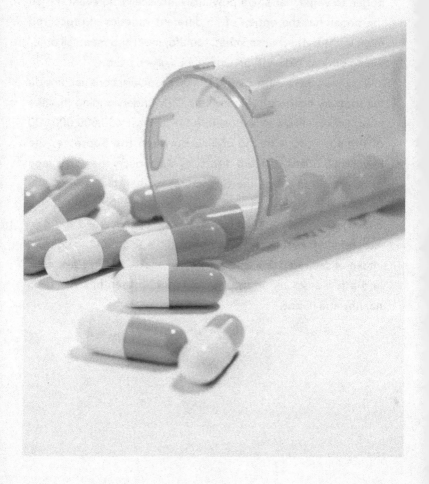

HEALTH AND WELLBEING

Getting huge

Gym attendance is a positive activity that can bring with it health and wellbeing benefits that extend across the lifespan, bogan or no. It's great for metabolism, bone density and blood pressure, but these factors are entirely unrelated to why the male bogan joins the gym. It's there to get HUGE. The bogan, with its poor coping skills and tendency to act impulsively, deeply feels the existential urge to become the alpha gladiator in the nightclub, both to catch the eye of the female bogan, and to become physically dominant over the other males. As with many other aspects of its life, it exhibits no subtlety or moderation; it craves the xtreme.

At the gym, the male bogan can generally be found near a mirror, dramatically swinging the largest dumbbells it can pick up. Rather than working on its entire physique, the bogan exclusively targets the parts of the body that can protrude from a tight Travisty t-shirt, creating an odd sense of proportion as its enormous, yet formless biceps dwarf other parts of its arms and torso. As a result, it can always be seen working out in a skimpy singlet, but loose pants.

The bogan's inability to resist an impossibly good shortcut will sometimes lead it to getting on the 'roids, which speed up the process of getting huge and reduce the amount of work required. The downsides, such as erectile dysfunction, testicular atrophy, paranoia and increased aggression are dismissed. Indeed, the bogan may lust after the increased aggression which can work well in tandem with its newly inflated massive guns. Once the bogan achieves a large size in the chest and biceps, it is then ready to apply its Ed Hardy and head to the nightclub with its comrades. Normally, someone who got this large would consider getting serious about

bodybuilding, but the dieting, lower body work and discipline required to earn a bodybuilder's lean physique are sacrifices a bogan is unwilling to make. Besides, if it can't instigate drunken brawls and then wolf down a souvlaki in a popular nightclub district, what's the point of getting huge in the first place?

Fad diets

While many bogans – usually the male ones – are busy getting huge at the gym, there are many more, of all stripes, getting huge by other means. Prominent among these are bogan standards like late-night McDonald's and KFC. However, there has been a shift underway in the bogan mindset.

Some time ago, the bogan became aware of the benefits of appearing healthy (as distinct from actually *being* healthy). This is because an aesthetically pleasing bogan is better positioned to be photographed in those unusual middle sections of the street presses whereby young bogans pose lasciviously in front of a stranger's camera at the club, often six Jagerbombs into a 12-Jagerbomb night.

The result of this change first manifested itself in the bogan stating loudly and publicly that it was 'watching its weight'. However, this had little to do with actually wanting to eat less-delicious foods. The response was nigh-on instant. McDonald's started a 'salads' range, with sufficient dressing as to make it resistant to ordinary forms of biodegradation. And Subway emerged, with foot-long (this is not just a marketing term) sandwiches, boasting 'six grams of fat'. What remained unmentioned was that the six-gram option was a half-sized sandwich, with wholemeal bread, no meat, no cheese, no sauce and no taste. Naturally, the bogan proceeded to order the foot-long meatball (double meat) with tasty cheese, BBQ sauce and pickles, then sat down to enjoy its healthy lunch. Only to top it off with six 'home style' double chocolate chip cookies.

The ensuing weight gain created significant consternation for bogans nationwide. Why was its new diet not successful? Why did it continue to register a BMI of 32? There were clearly only two options. For the male bogan, it was that it obviously boasted a higher-than-normal muscle mass, a conclusion reached after learning that professional athletes often had higher-than-normal BMI readings. The female, on the other hand, decided that it had malfunctioning lymph nodes. Or something similarly medicine-y sounding.

As a result, male bogans did nothing. Female bogans, with eyes fixed firmly on the prize, took to 'dieting'. For years, carbs were the enemy. The Atkins diet, which, not incidentally, advocated the massive consumption of fats in order to get thin, failed, because it failed to deal with the bogans' poor metabolism and/or lymph glands – or was it thyroids? So, suddenly, the diet market was awash with shakes. Sure Slim, Celebrity Slim and Tony Ferguson all promoted themselves as being able to reduce the collective bogan weight by a noteworthy proportion.

So bogans began drinking shakes. With their Subway and Macca's salads.

Functional water

In the last decade, two products making little sense but extracting exorbitant amounts of money from the bogan have proliferated on the shelves of Australian supermarkets. Item number one is water in a bottle. Although widely available from a tap for less than

1/2000th of the price, the bogan happily pays more for a litre of water than it does for a litre of petrol – because it's conveniently packaged in a shiny plastic bottle, and it has a brand.

The second is vitamins. Also in a bottle. Always looking for an easier but more expensive way of doing things, the bogan happily hands over $15–20 for a bottle of vitamin C, cold pressed fish oil or specially formulated emu's knob, despite the fact that most of these vitamins and minerals are present in everyday fresh food items or offer only spurious nutritional benefit. Vitamin pills promising vague but appealing outcomes such as 'vitality' appeal strongly to the hypochondria that many bogans selectively commandeer to attract attention. It should come as no surprise that the corporate junta's latest assault on the bogan hip pocket should combine these two bogan-approved products.

Enter 'functional water'. Water that does shit. Two thousand years after biblical literalists vow that water allowed an amazing prophet to walk on it, product marketers have risen to a god-like level by creating another amazing profit on it.

Not content with the astronomical profit margins and environmental damage incurred by bottled water, beverage manufacturers worked out that by adding red food colouring and supplements like 'dragonfruit' and 'triple antioxidants', they could charge the bogan 4000 times the price of tap water. With maxtreme names like 'power C' and 'triple X'* and promising seemingly magical properties, vitamin water promises the bogan incredible attributes such as endurance, power, and energy.

---

*   The link between products featuring the letter X and their popularity among bogans has been overwhelmingly proven at the TBL Institute by our crack team of German scientists.

After finally gaining traction with its massive cans, the Coca-Cola company is at the centre of the functional water heist. Its glacéau vitaminwater (replete with exotic Euro diacritic) product displays an alarming understanding of the bogan. The company has allocated some of the phenomenal profit margin to paying for product placement on *Sex and the City*, and getting bogan idols Jennifer Aniston and 50 Cent to endorse its product. It has also created a pointless Facebook group for the product, which the bogan may join to construct its brand-based identity.

The outcome of all of this can be seen at your local gym, where the male bogan is getting huge next to the female bogan who is getting tiny. Both of them are proudly carrying a $4.50 bottle of brightly coloured and branded water, empowered by the fact that 0.3 ml of dragonfruit will make their bogan dreams come true.

Melanin

The bogan will not be able to offer you a definition of what melanin is, despite being extremely interested in the topic. What it is, is a class of compounds found in plants and animals, and the bogan also finds it at the beach. Bogans of both genders have been known to remain at the beach for hours at a time seeking melanin, sometimes walking around purposely, sometimes lying motionless in patient wait for the imminent discolouration. By the end of the day, the sunburnt bogan has usually managed to acquire some melanin, along with a few wrinkles.

Forever on the lookout for a quicker, more xpensive, more xtreme way to accomplish a task, many bogans turned to tanning lounges in the 1990s to get their hit of melanin. They would pay

$20 to lie in a plastic tube and get blasted by lamps. The pungent smell of coconut oil and burning human flesh constituted a dizzying reward for the newly bronzed bogan, and they returned again and again. This continued until about five years ago, when young St Kilda local Clare Oliver spent too much time in tanning lounges, developed a melanoma, and engaged in a publicity process to warn bogans that their melanin cravings were potentially fatal. She died in 2007 aged 26, and her message got through to many bronzed bogans.

In the three years that followed, the number of solariums in Australia declined by a third, but the bogan's desire to be bronzed did not decline at all. The shift in bronzing tastes coincided with a proliferation of spray tans, creams and lotions. These eagerly purchased fake tanning products come with the promise of transforming pale bogans into the colour of 'ethnic ' people that they do not like. This oddly contradictory aspirational racism is rarely effective, with the bogan ending up a blotchy shade of orange. Often, the bogan will attempt to combine a day at the beach with the excessive application of fake tan, creating vast tracts of visible orange flesh (often punctuated by tramp stamps and tribal tattoos). Some of the more striking markings of the bronze-hungry bogan are the much dreaded 'Vegemite knees', acquired when the poor application of a poor fake tan product results in a series of dark brown creases at the joints, presumably rich in vitamin B . . . for bogan.

Spurious allergies

The bogan likes to elicit reactions. Not content with ignoring the symptoms suggestive of a sexually transmitted infection, it effortlessly occupies its mind with its multitudinous allergies. Allergies are acquired reactions to normally innocuous substances that are unique to an individual's immune system. Despite this inescapable medical construct, the bogan's allergies magically mirror those of Angelina Jolie, Bec Cartwright or pretty much anyone on the cover of *New Idea*. With a similar unpredictability to Axel Whitehead's belt buckle, in a given week the bogan might decide it's allergic to everything from peanuts to dairy to logic. This, despite having eaten a Picnic bar earlier in the day that was washed down with a chocolate Big M while driving its car. This curious brand of hypochondria may be attributed to its flawed understanding of biology but is in fact due to its rabid obsession with stupidity.

The bogan will also eagerly lap up any 'scientific study' its meandering eyes happen upon and as a result adopt its allergy for the week. If drinking coffee increases hypertension on Monday, it will be assured that drinking coffee will cure diabetes by Thursday. Adding to its allergic arsenal, the bogan was once told by *Today Tonight* that there might be a vague connection between obesity and one's thyroid gland. Months later when it finds itself hopelessly fat and asthmatic, it will tell its friends that this new-found obesity was due to a dysfunctional thyroid gland acquired at birth. And blame its stupid parents for giving it inferior organs.

Failing to establish the link between its tinea and lack of hygiene, the bogan will infer that the fungal infection is in fact a result of a food that it does not like. It will then loudly scowl at the unsuspecting Asian waiter at La Porchetta's because he failed to enquire about any existing food allergies. Even though it did not exist at the time of ordering. As Kelly quivers under the weight of her own delusions, she's ready to dig into two kilos of spaghetti bolognese, her gluten allergy notwithstanding.

Plus-size models

Despite its rigorous adherence to fad diets, once-a-month personal training sessions and watching *The Biggest Loser*, the bogan is getting fatter. This displeases the female bogan, who, with only so much leeway in blaming her failing thyroid gland, needs to look for other remedies for this ongoing existential bogan angst. In short, the bogan does not look like Nicole Ritchie, and is confused. The ultimate conclusion any self-respecting bogan would reach is to adapt her reality to make herself normal.

However, it is not the bogan who makes this leap, but *OK!* magazine (so named as to reassure the bogan that she is, indeed, OK!). Upon facing flagging sales and interest in its ever-widening array of not-so-wide celebrities on the cover, it takes a different tack. 'Real Women!' screams the biannual cover, as the editors divine that the bogan wants to be told that she, and people like her, are just as beautiful as professional models. These new photographic targets are dubbed 'plus-size models' and 'real women', and offer the fiercely anti-PC bogan an opportunity to selectively embrace a form of political correctness that legitimises her own robust form.

Roused from her inward-looking misery, the bogan can purchase the magazine in question and gaze on these women who look 'just like me', and begin loudly proclaiming to all and sundry that they 'Want to see *real* women!' After the success of *OK!*, the bogan finds herself confronted with sundry images of Magda Szubanski, celebrating and revelling in her diminished level of fatness yet remaining a 'real woman'. Thus validated, the bogan can continue applying copious amounts of mayonnaise to her McDonald's salads. She's a real woman.

Despite this pronouncement, the following week Lara Bingle and Jennifer Hawkins are splashed across the covers of every major women's mag in the country to massively increased sales. The bogan, as she peruses the collection in front of her, picking up Angelina Jolie, Jessica Alba (who is back to her pre-baby weight) and an oddly emaciated Rebecca Twigley, continues to talk to her cohorts about how she wishes to see 'real women' in magazines. She then forgets.

Two years later, *OK!* decides that it needs to 'pay tribute to the real women', and puts out a cover with a suburban housewife, discussing her battles with body image.

The male bogan is mortified.

ADHD

The bogan's desire for glory manifests itself in many different ways. There's the uninformed gambling, the process of getting huge, the killing of things, and so much more. All of this glory-hunting takes up significant slices of the bogan's time, so the bogan is prone to taking shortcuts on other things to ensure that it can fit in the viewing of a Twenty/Twenty cricket game before going to the pub to watch a cover band butcher 'Sex on Fire'. One of the things that regularly gets short-changed by the bogan is the adequate raising of its children.

Due to neglect, a massive can for breakfast each day, and impulsive and anti-intellectual parental role models, the bogán's children are quite likely to behave like uncontrollable morons.

While the bogan parent is always eager to acquire cheap glory, it is vehemently unwilling to accept responsibility for the conduct of bogan junior, despite little Bilynda and Maxxx busily setting fire to the upholstery in the formal dining area. Using the same mental shortcut that caused it to decide that it had a spurious gluten allergy, the bogan will loudly and arbitrarily declare that its recalcitrant offspring has ADHD. At this point, the bogan parent feels relieved and reassured that none of this mess is its fault.

The calmness and relief is short lived, however, because parent-teacher interviews are very stressful for the bogan parent. Faced with professionally trained opinions on its child's behaviour, rage surges through the bogan's veins like fuel through a jet ski. It decides that because bogan junior can do no wrong, the teacher needs to be taken down a peg or two, in the process gaining much-needed exposure to the bogan's 'real world'. The teacher rudely suggests that the child might not have ADHD and could perhaps benefit from better guidance and support. The teacher also suggests getting a medical opinion on the alleged ADHD, which is interpreted by the bogan parent as a statement of doubt that the bogan might not be a medical expert. This is unacceptable to the bogan. Amid the screeching, the finger pointing, the feigned shock and the threats of retribution, the bogan parent will variously assign blame to the other students, other parents, the teacher, or the fundamental concept of education. It will eventually storm out, vowing to itself that it will craft its child even more closely in its own image.

At a subsequent BBQ, the bogan will proudly regale all attending about the time they stuck it up the headmaster. It will describe in vivid detail its every unreasonable conclusion and pathetic excuse that justified its spawn interrupting and assaulting 30 other innocent children stupidly focused on obtaining an education.

Slater & Gordon

Years of watching _Today Tonight_ and _A Current Affair_ and reading News Limited have taught the bogan that it is not to blame for anything. The introduction of a kaleidoscope of alternative scapegoats for the faults and failings of bogan society – foreigners, children, foreigners' children – have placed the bogan in a warm, soothing cocoon of impenetrable security. Their child's illness is an allergy. Their resulting behaviour is a disease treatable by anti-psychotics. Job loss is the result of cheap migrant labour. There is no action the bogan can take that will result in negative consequences or blame for the bogan. Chlamydia often has no symptoms.

Akin to Max Markson, who saw the bogan need to be famous and monetised it, like Coke saw the bogan need for massive cans and monetised it, Slater & Gordon realised – well before most – the bogan desire for xtreme lawyering. The bogan lives life to the maxtreme, but when something fucks up, it wants justice – the mega justice that comes from a legal system to the power of maximum times awesome. Should a bogan slip on a puddle of spilt detergent at the supermarket as the pimply 16-year-old fetches a mop, the supermarket faces xtreme bogan legal retribution. Should a bogan forget how to properly operate its jet ski and do its back in, water speed regulations are at fault. Should a bogan fail at a glassing attempt and get hurt, their assailant is a heinous criminal who deserves righteous dispensation of legal vengeance forthwith. And when it happens, Slater & Gordon provide the mega justice.

Even better, they do it for nothing.

Just like Harvey Norman and their ilk realised that if the bogan has nothing to pay upfront they will walk out of any store with an inordinate amount of televisual and refrigeration equipment they do not need, Slater & Gordon's epiphany was that, offered free legal advice, the bogan will sue anyone for anything, at anytime. The bogan only pays legal fees if they win their case.

So, despite the bogan's firm belief that several years of watching *Law & Order* have prepared it for the rigours of the Australian courtroom, S&G are there to represent it. The bogan hates rules and laws, but is not aware that the existence of many of the rules it hates most is a direct result of its own reckless behaviour. S&G are aware.

Wii Fit

There is a long, prestigious roster of ridiculous items that the bogan can be convinced to purchase. If the bogan is thirsty, it will not merely drink water, it will crave a Boost Juice smoothie or a functional water (actually cordial). If the bogan wishes to leech some cultural cachet from the bloated corpses of Bach and Sinatra, it will try to illegally download some André Rieu or Michael Bublé (actually a Canadian dwarf), before realising it doesn't know what a torrent is, and buy it at JB Hi Fi. Of course, the bogan wishes to get fit and lose inches (never centimetres) off its waist, so it spent years embracing the Assmaster 5000 or some other nonsense. But in the modern age, buying strangely contrived exercise equipment over the phone seems a bit antiquated. The savvy bogan wants to move beyond late-night exercise tools, to something state-of-the-art.

Nintendo saw this and Nintendo acted. Add to this illustrious list of amazingly pointless products, that in combination account for 40% of the Australian economy, the Wii Fit. With the Wii Fit, the bogan discovered an incredible new means of being ridiculous. And loved it. By the end of 2009, 800,000 Wii Fit consoles had been sold to bogans across Australia, as they realised that by standing on a plastic platform watching television and barely moving, they would lose weight and tone up.

Now, while the bogan is busily not consuming carbohydrates through a straw, it wobbles unsteadily on its cankles, looking for all the world to be swatting imaginary flies or some such, as poorly animated characters move at random on a five-second delay on an 89-inch plasma screen. Having justified a quick return journey to the McDonald's drive-through to pick up a few thousand kilojoules , the bogan can then work on increasing their Facebook IQ score by exercising their underutilised grey matter on Big Brain Academy: Wii Degree. Here, the bogan engages in arithmetic and problem-solving tasks aimed at eight-year-olds, and sits back smugly when it manages to outscore five-year-old Rylan. This Wii thing does make the bogan smarter. Oh, and fitter too.

MATING
AND
PR⬤CREATING

Weddings: the courtship

She was already in white when they met. It was serendipity. Their eyes locked across the cavernous room that housed Sensation™ White at 3 am. It was hard to look away. This was, in part, due to the extreme dilation of their pupils. He began to walk across the room, before accidentally shouldering some guy called Lance, who took umbrage at his inability to navigate a swarming sea of pristine, Napisan-ed bogans, and tried to glass him with his half-empty Corona bottle. Eventually he finds her, and they fall into each other's arms. They share their thoughts on how loud the music is, and how fucked they are.

Flash forward two years, and they stand silently, downcast, in his parents' en suite, staring morbidly at the home pregnancy test as the litmus stick turns a sinister shade of blue.

Flash forward another month, and they sit in the audience of *Deal Or No Deal*. During the ad break, Andrew O'Keefe wanders over to where they sit and addresses the couple, under the guise of generic crowd banter. Suddenly, his expression changes, and a glint appears in his eyes. He takes a hand from each and places one in the other. The bogan male falls to his knees, fishes around in his jacket pocket, and retrieves a purple (velvet) jewellery box.

A.O'K glances mischievously at her and says, 'Aaron, is there something you want to tell Erin?', as the bogan stares earnestly at her. 'Yes, Andrew. There is. Erin, I've loved you ever since we locked eyes at Sensation™. Will you be my beautiful wife?' She stands, hands to her mouth, as the crowd chants 'Deal! Deal!' She says yes. Tears are shed as A.O'K struts back triumphantly to his lectern and announces, on national television, that his guests are now betrothed, to rapturous applause. To this moment, it is the high point of both of their short lives.

The camera zooms in, focusing on the glittering stone newly placed on Erin's ring finger. It is a shining clear gem, the size of her pupils all those years ago. After the cameras have stopped rolling, she says, 'Forget cut, colour and clarity . . . I just want carat!' The male, meanwhile, has descended into an insolvent abyss as he contemplates the alarming synchronicity of the ring's repayment schedule with that of his plasma screen TV.

Weddings: the preparations

The bogan bride, shortly after cementing the ring to her finger, begins to consider the import of her decision. She's getting married! Dedicating her life to another human being, building a life together – house, children, the works. But more importantly, she has a wedding to organise!

It can be daunting for the bogan – where to start? Invariably, she turns to the same oracles that have answered her questions for much of her life. How many gut rolls does Britney have? Is Amy Winehouse back on the horse? And how the hell do I go about organising my wedding?!

Flipping through the magazine, she spies the latest celebrity event: Rove and Tasma, resplendent in their finery. She is aware that Rove was married on a remote Western Australian beach, but as her new mother-in-law has recently found god, it is best that the event takes place in a church.

However, as the bride-to-be flips through the pages of 'candid' photos and exposed snatches of celebs alighting from limos, she realises she wants to be classy. So she goes to the newsagent and forks out around $200 for six issues of *Aussie Bride* magazine or some such – her new bible.

Page by page, the dream wedding takes shape. There will be matching lavender ties on the groomsmen, perfectly accompanying the bridesmaids' dresses. The bridal train will be six carriages long, the better to conceal a substantial caboose (better hit the SureSlim to take care of that), and because longer is better. The same value system applies to the bridal vehicle. A wedding of this magnitude requires nothing less than an adapted military vehicle. Yes, a gangsta black stretch Hummer limousine is what Posh and Becks would have wanted.

The reception will be something special too. Caviar is ordered, and the money has already been paid by the time someone discovers it is fish eggs. Not to worry, the guests could wash it down with some champagne. The bogan has discovered an expensive but remarkably successful ingredient that makes indifferent bubbly taste twice as exquisite – a Moët label. The entire afternoon will be overseen by Danny 'DJ' Johnson, spinning his favourites while wearing sunglasses. He assures the groom that his iPod wedding playlist can generate 'My Sharona' and 'Call on Me' up to three times per hour.

Meanwhile, the bridal party is a seething mess. The bridesmaids dresses are all wrong. The fat one looks frumpy in it, and the skinny one wants to choose something more strappy. In a heady rush of self-importance, the skinny one storms off, abandoning her post. She is replaced by a portly understudy, who looks worse still in the newly strapless number.

This turmoil takes its toll on the bride-to-be. Realising that her magazine did not prepare her for this catfight, the bridal freakout occurs. Months of avoiding solid food at her dressmaker's insistence has rendered her unstable. She medicates her anxiety with a panic binge consisting of carbohydrates, glucose, egocentrism and streaked mascara. The big day draws ever nearer.

BuX/hen's nights

Following the financially and emotionally crippling odyssey that is the bridal freakout, the bogan moves on to the most awaited part of its nuptials. While the bridesmaids in a bogan wedding often fall victim to the tyrannical tantrums and hysterical breakdowns of their new overlord, one (usually the loudest and most single) will take the heat due to one simple privilege it grants them: the opportunity to anoint themselves the architect of the most important night of the process in their eyes: 'OhmygodOhmygodOhmygod'. That's right, the hen's night.

This is the bridesmaid's chance to assert her newly held belief that her single life is far, far superior to being wed. It is her time to shine, and her chance to prove it by organising a spastic orgy of ridiculous, 'sexy' games, resulting in the bride-to-be dirty dancing with random strangers at a random CBD pub before passing out in a pool of her own vomit in the cab on the way home . . .

But, to backtrack a bit, this tendency is not isolated to the *bride's* friends. A long-held male bogan truism is that, upon becoming married, the sex dries up. Notwithstanding that it may be because they no longer deem it necessary to engage in foreplay beyond 'You awake?', this fear, rarely mentioned among actually married bogans, has become acknowledged fact. Hence, the bogan buck's night became synonymous with strippers. The best man will apply all of his limited imagination to the task of organising a special and unique event. One painful hour of thinking later, the piece of paper in front of him containing only a giant X, a fiery skull and a doodle of a stick figure performing fellatio on another stick figure, he decides to copy Troy's buck's idea from a fortnight ago: paintball, pub and strippers.

The groom-to-be's friends loudly rally around the groom-to-be, bringing to his attention the impermanence of his sexual freedom with chants of 'Go on, it's your last night as a free and single man, so don't be a poof and let Candi do whatever she wants to you.' Candi, spurred on by his inert curiosity, will proceed to prepare him for married life by covering him in cream and trying to shove a dildo up his bum.

Not to be outdone, however, the female bogan, in the name of 'feminism', decided that anything the blokes can do, they can do bigger, dirtier, smellier and lamer. All while wearing a feather boa, a ridiculous sash and pink plastic tiara. And drinking Bacardi through a straw that is hilariously shaped like a – wait for it – penis! Bogan bridesmaids have thus identified a plethora of methods to humiliate and degrade this peculiar brand of poultry. By booking a two-hour session where the hen can 'learn sexy new moves' by repeatedly falling off a pole, the hen's night is a curious inversion of the buck's night aesthetic – men ogling at women turning into women wanting to be ogled by men.

The key message of the evening is that it's the last chance that the bogan will ever get to party. This is despite the fact that the bogan remains irresponsible and impulsive for most of its lifespan, and is quite likely to divorce and experience at least one additional buck's/hen's night in its name in the future.

With this ritual dutifully carried out, the bogans are now ready to marry.

Weddings: her big day

Saturday morning, 11 am. The bride is 15 minutes late, just as she planned it. She is ready for HER day. The groom and his five men stand in their rented suits with lavender cravats and pocket handkerchiefs ($1500) looking generically awkward/nervous, just as she planned. The bridal car arrives – a stretch Hummer ($2000) – makes a fifteen-point turn in order to get in the church's ($5000) driveway. The bride and her five maids spill out, each tripping over in an effort to avoid stepping on her strapless, yet veiled, gown ($5500). They stand, waiting, freezing in the (unplanned) bad weather in their unnecessarily short lavender dresses ($2500), each with skin an incandescent orange hue, their hair ($400) and makeup ($300) struggling to remain in place in the biting wind and driving rain.

As the iPod attached behind the scenes begins playing 'One' by U2, she appears, radioactive in her luminescence ($50), in the doorway. She then waits 15 minutes more while her retinue paces slowly, sonorously down the aisle one at a time in intervals predetermined by Jenny, the wedding planner ($2000). But first, the 'adorable' niece and nephew potter aimlessly down to the altar, confusedly tossing flowers in every which direction while drooling on their custom-made tuxedo ($300) and dress ($500). Speaking of flowers, bridesmaid #4 left hers in the Hummer, and dashes out to get them ($400).

Eventually, relishing in the incessant flash of her friends' and family's SLR bulbs, she arrives at the altar, a queer look of joy and resolute determination on her face. Her beau, and his accompanying entourage, are the embodiment of the opposite of their behaviour a week earlier – at the buck's – as they cheerfully stand by and watch their mate cry like a little girl (just as she planned) as the music swells, the cameras point in his direction and the videographer ($2000) zooms in.

The priest ($400) smiles benignly on his supplicants, and begs them to sit. The bride is glad as she hasn't eaten for four days and is feeling woozy. The priest then begins to invoke his bog-standard collection of platitudes for the massed horde, which laps them up enthusiastically. The fifth bridesmaid and groomsman, left with no jobs to do, are asked to undertake the readings, which are lifted from a list of possible readings offered by the priest, hence have no actual relationship to either bride or groom, as neither are really Christian. They do so, in the stilted, singsong manner of those who have rehearsed studiously, yet struggle to pronounce 'begat'.

However, the bride is insistent that their wedding be 'different'. At first, this causes some consternation, as, when pressed, neither party can conceive of how to achieve this. Until she stumbles upon the idea of personalised vows in her fifth issue of *Aussie Bride* ($18.95). They spend minutes each googling furiously the best words they can steal from other people to develop their own special vows. Several minutes of 'loves' and 'I will always put away the dishes'-style 'vows' later, the priest smiles benignly once again, asks the obligatory questions, receives the obligatory answers.

After the formalities are completed, the party moves outside and greetings are made. Then the bridal party vanishes, along with its extended family, for the five-hour session of photographs ($7000) in various locales. During this time, the guests return to their cars to drive for an hour to the remote winery where the reception ($200 per head = $40,000) is to be held. The guests arrive (petrol = $40, accommodation = $200), and dutifully place their gifts from the registry ($50–$5000) on the allocated table. When the in-laws all arrive, they gently prod each other to discover which family spent more on the BBQ/dining set/honeymoon suite, until one father learns what he believes to be the truth, and struts off with a self-satisfied smirk.

The reception hall, clad entirely in white and featuring a four-piece jazz band ($2000), is full of tired, bored guests, waiting for the bar to open by the time the couple and their crew arrive.

Another 45 minutes later, the entire bridal party have been introduced and seated, and the eating and drinking begin in earnest. The cake ($1000) is cut before it collapses under its own weight. The dance (to Michael Bublé's version of 'Moondance') is danced. The groom's uncle falls asleep in the corner. The fifth groomsman – the bride's weird younger brother who no one really likes – has been sent to sit in the car after he touched up the maid of honour. The fathers-in-law have come to fisticuffs after one reneged on his responsibility to cover half of the $75,000 bill for the day. The bride, before leaving, tosses the bouquet. The ladies present make their obligatory gestures towards not wanting to stand in the pack before surreptitiously muscling others out of the way in an effort to walk away the victor. The men present take careful note of which participants are most aggressive . . .

Finally, the groom carries his new bride upstairs to their suite for the night. Finally, after her day has run itself out, he can have HIS moment. He can nail a chick in a wedding dress. She falls asleep as he disrobes. Just like she planned it. He taps her on the shoulder, and says, 'You awake?' She doesn't stir. He contemplates doing it anyway.

Faux lesbianism

Almost everything the bogan does revolves around drawing attention to itself. Be it the highest hair, the most garish t-shirt, the most fluorescent laces on its shiny new Dunlop Volleys, the biggest guns or the largest sunglasses, the bogan is living a constant audition to be a contestant on *Big Brother*. More specifically, however, the bogan has a narrower focus on attracting the attention of the opposite sex.

As this sartorial and behavioural arms race continues to escalate, ambitious bogans are being forced to revert to ever-more outrageous activities in order to stand out. While the male bogan continues to embrace sheer muscular bulk and gaudy attire, its female counterpart has realised that the male couldn't give two shits about what she was wearing. She had to stand out by emphasising her sexual availability.

This is not as easy as it once was. In the early days, it was a simple matter of wearing revealing clothes, which is harmless enough. Then came the commodification of *Playboy*, entrenching in the bogan mind a notion of the feminine ideal spawned from the syphilis-ridden mind of an 83-year-old Lothario. But shortly thereafter, bogans discovered internet porn, and Pandora's box was well and truly opened. Suddenly, the male bogan's definition of 'sexy' devolved to one of two definitions: 'fake-tittied blonde copping a tag team from a pair of oversized bouncers/porn stars' or 'chicks making out/strapping on'. In the absence of societal acceptance of breaking out sex toys in public, bogan girls began slamming their tongues down each others' throats with an enthusiasm that their potential paramours found all the more intoxicating for its insecurity and desperation. The male bogan even found a second benefit, as it could now appear to accept homosexuality without ever having to condone two guys, you know, doing it.

Today, the faux-lesbian encounter tends to happen about five cruisers into a ten-cruiser-and-half-bottle-of-Jack-Daniels night. The bogan male, stalking its appealingly tandem prey, waits until many more of those ten cruisers have disappeared before making its move. Gently, wordlessly, he guides the now-malleable faux-lesbian femme bogans to an upstairs bedroom, before attempting to perform an (albeit confusing) one-man Chinese finger trap on one or both. All too often, the evening ends with the male bogan covertly performing the Stranger* on itself in a nearby carpark.

Massive perambulators

The bogan likes to procreate. Its desire to simultaneously possess and devour its cake has resulted in furious, ill-advised spawning. With the federal government providing replacement cake in the form of the baby bonus, bogans have brought about a malaise that has had far-reaching effects across the political and social landscape of the country. A traffic jam of bogan offspring has been unleashed onto the unsuspecting world, one Mercedes and McLaren at a time. While bogan progeny are mostly harmless until the age of three, they do require assistance to be transported prior to developing fully functional walking skills. And the only way a bogan's baby may travel is via the biggest, loudest and

---

* As explained on page 273.

most xtreme form of baby conveyance – a massive, 'fuck-off, we're fertile' pram.

Mumma Hummers, as they are affectionately known, are the armoured tanks of the baby transport world, the M1 Abrams of the toddler moving universe. These giant infant carriers ruthlessly dominate every footpath, zebra crossing and foodcourt aisle that they happen to rumble across. Should a stray pedestrian or non-xtreme pram cross their path, the victim is likely to be subjected to the bogan's perspective on parenthood.

'I'm fucking outraged. I blame this whole thing on the bloody government. First, they tell us to have more bloody kids because Peter Costello said to have one for Australia, and we'll get five grand for free. Of course, those rip-off artists didn't tell us how expensive kids are, or that I will put on weight and can't bloody drink sav blonc for a year.'

While the bogan could have obtained a perfectly serviceable pram and other accessories for a fifth of the price, products that don't allow for xtreme child rearing are not realistic alternatives. The massive $2450 pram allows the bogan to endow itself with ungodly levels of parental territoriality, and includes technology adapted from the space shuttle. For while the bogan mother is walking a child instead of a pit bull, she desires to intimidate all the same. Soon, a clever designer will realise the commercial possibilities of covering the side of prams with tribal tattoo designs and toothsome horned animals.

Footy trips

While its mating patterns have been mentioned before, there exists an interesting anomaly in bogan behaviour. In the months of

September and October, a migration of bogan males of breeding age occurs as the weather begins to grow warmer. But instead of flying south to more temperate climes, flocks of footy playing bogans will board a Jetstar bogan bus and migrate northwards towards the tropics. After having spent the winter months foraging for a leather ball, the bogan male is now ready to dedicate all of its time to binge drinking and rutting.

Flocks of southern bogans fly to different tropical breeding grounds, with some flocks returning to the very same site year after year. Large footy-trip breeding grounds are found in Byron Bay, Surfers Paradise, Noosa, and as far north as Bali and Phuket. While the bogan's ancestors came to many of these places to breed, the bogan has recently had to adapt to the changing conditions. The availability of exotic fruits such as rohypnol, ecstasy and tequila slammers has caused the bogan's feeding habits to change, as has the advent of higher perching sites – some up to 60 storeys high. The male bogan has been known to feed these fruits to females on its perch, fulfilling its role as hunter gatherer.

While some things have changed, some have not. The availability of water is crucial to bogan breeding, causing intense pecking and glassing among footy-tripping bogan males in coastal areas to secure the best breeding sites. The presence of flock members named Hammer, Jonno, Shagger, Tank and Spider has also been a constant for generations of bogan males. The bogan who is able to mate with the most females is generally anointed as leader. These attempts at bareback mating will continue throughout the night, with varying levels of success.

Like a bee dancing the details of the whereabouts of pollen to the rest of its hive, the footy-tripping bogan reports in vivid detail its mating attempts to the rest of its migratory flock. This behaviour is evolving, however, with many bogan males now using mobile phones to record themselves or other members of their flock mating. The footage is displayed to the rest of the flock, in all its flapping and squawking glory. Many footy-tripping bogans possess breeding partners back near their winter foraging grounds, and these partners are not, under any circumstances, permitted to learn of the happenings at the October breeding site. To prevent this from occurring, the footy-tripping bogans have devised a special call to each other; 'what happens on tour stays on tour'. If a member of the flock breaks this code, they are banished and forced to seek mating partners without the assistance of the pack.

At the conclusion of its annual week-long period in the tropics, the sunburnt, liver-damaged, and gonorrhoea-afflicted bogan will take wing once more, and return south. It will arrive back at the nest of its normal mating partner, who will nurture the male back to health over the following 11 months.

The Brisbane Broncos

On 3 July 2009, the male bogan was happily nestled on its interest-free couch, watching the Broncos v Warriors game on the plasma and nursing a beer. 'Baaaaaybe?' came a voice from six rooms away in the kitchen of the McMansion. The bogan continued to watch the game, and barked at Israel Folau's fumble of the ball. 'Baaaaaaaybe?' came the voice again. At the next commercial break, the male bogan responded. 'What?'

'We need to talk, babe,' declared the female bogan, knowing full well that the game was still underway at Suncorp Stadium. While the male bogan didn't know this, its partner had been on the same interest-free couch the previous evening, watching *A Current Affair*. The female hadn't slept well that night. Irritated at being pulled away from the plasma, the male trudged through the study, then through the formal dining room, then the lounge, library and meals room, eventually joining the female at the kitchen table. 'What?'

'Babe, I've been thinking. I want to start a family. I was wa–' The male cut her off, fear in his eyes.

'WHAT?!?'

The female bogan yelled back, demanding to be allowed to continue. 'As I bloody said, I was watching *A Current Affair* last night.'

'So?' replied the male, aware that the commercial break back in the rumpus room would be ending within the next few seconds.

'Well, as of two days ago, the baby bonus is worth like a grand more than it was a couple of years back.'

The male bogan's face softened. In its private moments, it had often thought to itself that it might like to be a father one day. It wasn't entirely happy with the size of its plasma screen, and it paused to consider whether it would finally be able to convince the female of the need to upgrade it, but that conversation would have to wait.

'Oh, babe,' it gushed, leaning forward to embrace the female bogan. They remained in each other's arms for what seemed like an eternity. 'What do you think of Tyarnee?' asked the female politely.

'Nah, it'll be a little bloke . . . Tysenn.' Not even differences of opinion like this could come between them now.

Later that evening, the bogan male went to buy two bottles of

Moët to celebrate with, and the pair of them discussed extending the McMansion to include a nursery, a kids' rumpus, and a cubbyhouse with an Xbox and plasma. 'Oh, I can't wait to use the baby bonus to shop for Armani Junior!' enthused the female bogan.

'Do they make Broncos jerseys?' its partner replied.

Richard Mercer

The bogan will tell you that, unlike the non-bogan, it has an innate and entire grasp of the 'real world'. The bogan's real world contains heaps of things bogans like, such as road rage, killing things and interest free finance for enormous plasma screens. But, being the real world, sometimes there are also things that bogans do not at all like. Arguably the foremost downside of the real world is the bogan's exposure to the consequences of its ill-considered actions. Oftentimes, the bogan calls on the government to 'do something'. The rest of the time, it calls on Richard Mercer.

From 8 pm to midnight Sunday to Thursday, Richard's baritone words are on hand to sooth the anxious bogan in the form of his successful radio show *Love Song Dedications*. How was the bogan to know that cheating on its boyfriend with its boyfriend's brother was going to jeopardise its relationship? All the bogan knows is that it wants everything back to normal, and that Richard is the central plank in this restorative process. All the bogan needs to do is call Richard, wail disjointedly on the radio for 20 seconds, and then Richard will unveil his chocolatey tones to announce that everything in the real world will turn out just fine. This modern day version of a church confessional comes with the added bogan broadcast bonus of airing its dirty laundry to a wider audience than is possible at the pub.

After being informed by Richard that 'it sounds like you really do care for him', the bogan agrees blubberingly and awaits the first bars of 'How Am I Supposed To Live Without You' by Michael Bolton. It knows that its penance has been served, and that it is only a matter of time before the estranged lover comes scuttling back into its lecherous arms. It does not occur to the bogan that there is an infinitesimally small chance that the intended recipient is actually listening to the show, and that it's far more likely that they're out on the prowl for someone who isn't idiotic enough to think that Richard Mercer's velvet-coated dungeon is a valuable diplomatic instrument.

Meanwhile, Richard ploughs on, his unbreakable job security underpinned by the tens of thousands of bogans whose decision-making skills make them ticking time bombs for desperate love song dedications down the track. Dubbed the 'Love God' by listeners and the Mix FM network of broadcasters, this luckless deity is consigned to a weekly 20-hour dosage of bogan hell for all eternity.

MULTI-CULTURALISM

Prefacing racist statements with 'I'm not racist but . . .'

The bogan is a beacon of tolerance. This comes from the brief association with a person from a different country/race/religion at the local Thai or Chinese takeaway, the ostracised work colleague, or the evening spent on the Coronas with a mate's girlfriend's friend's Asian friend. Thus, in the event of a discussion relating to racism, Aboriginals or Asian drivers, the bogan is all knowing.

Each statement typically begins with an honest admission such as:

'I'm not racist . . . but those Abos really have it too good, the bastards.'

Or:

'I'm not racist . . . but those fucking curries should quit whining. Seriously, a couple of them get bashed and you'd think it was the end of the world.'

This form of disclaimer can be extended beyond occasional interactions with foreigners, and many bogans will actively carry, wear or enact visible or tangible evidence of their god-given right to besmirch those who differ from them. Common examples include Buddhist iconography – in the form of home furnishings, or the more portable keychain – t-shirts emblazoned with foreign languages, or tattoos with bad translations of common phrases in languages of countries it hates. The bogan can equally smear different religions (Muslims) and lifestyles (the Gays). A similar variant to the 'I'm not racist, but . . .' prefix is the 'Some of my best friends are [insert subject of vilification], but . . .' This not only provides the bogan with the high horse of moral certitude, but the appearance of impartiality. The bogan, in its suffocating cocoon of intolerance, believes that lying about its gay friends (it has none) gives it special licence to attack, because it knows them so well.

By proudly displaying in this fashion, the bogan carries a semi-permanent signifier that, when they ruthlessly and unnecessarily characterise an entire billion-strong ethnic group on the basis of a tired stereotype, they do it from a position of understanding and empathy.

Contiki tours

In the 21st century, the bogan is no longer only interested in its town, the nearest beach and the occasional trip to Queensland. While it remains suspicious of other cultures, it wants to see the world, pose with different foreign label beers and sleep with as many (white) foreigners as it can. Enter the Contiki tour.

Contiki, and companies like it, package up overseas experiences so that the bogan can satisfy all of these needs. Up to 60 bogans are loaded into a bus at the airport, and are then whisked around for the next fortnight, vomiting in a different part of a new country each day. The bogan is able to physically witness many landmarks it has seen on television, and participate in hilarious 'holding up the leaning tower' style photos. Over and over and over again. All without the dreaded need to problem solve, learn or communicate with locals.

The tour company, meanwhile, organises every meal, bed, transfer and drinking location, while supervising and micro-managing every moment. This leaves the bogan to do what it does best – create a boorish, ignorant vortex that ruins the location for anyone else who happens to be there, and make clumsy attempts to fornicate with other members of the tour group. With rarely more than 24 hours spent in one city, Contiki ably caters to the short attention span and one-dimensional needs of the new bogan.

Now that Contiki has recently commenced offering all-inclusive tours through South East Asia, the bogan is now able to visit a whole array of countries in the region previously off limits. Hence, the male bogan can now be seen in his home town with a wider array of foreign beer-branded singlets than ever before, impressing the female bogan with his new sense of cosmopolitanism, worldliness and sexually transmitted diseases. The female too is more worldly, thanks to the purchase of an oriental themed home furnishing, acquired after haggling and berating a street vendor for ten minutes to save 40 cents.

Locally produced, foreign label beer

A Crown Lager used to be enough to make the bogan look sophisticated. The 'golden microphone' was in the right hand whenever a birthday speech, awards speech or other special occasion occurred. Crown was first released to the Australian public to commemorate the Queen's visit in 1954, allowing the bogan's ancestors to seem more classy for Her Highness. But globalisation (and, perhaps, republicanism) has meant that the new bogan needs more. It now wants to communicate its national sophistication by drinking beers from other countries.

Initially, the two main local brewers (Foster's and Lion Nathan) were fearful. If the new bogan didn't want to drink local beers as much, how would they make money? After much hand-wringing and whiteboard scribbling, an answer appeared. The approach was made: 'Dear European brewery, can we please get permission to make beer in Australia, pay you so we can put your label on it, and sell it to our bogans?' If the price was right, the answer was often 'Yes'. Or 'Ja!', as the case may be.

And so it happened. Soon the shelves of the local bottle shop were seeing more Carlsberg, Beck's, Stella Artois and Heineken than ever before. And cheaper than it previously was, too. Now the new bogan could get his hands on a slab of European beer for under $45, and gain all of the credibility that a slender green bottle could confer. New bogan males wanted to be him, bogan females wanted to be with him. One night he was trying to pick up at a backpackers bar, and his international style caught the eye of a German girl. He bought her a stylish beer, which she spat out on the first sip, exclaiming, 'Zis is not Beck's!' Correct analysis, Gretchen, the primary thing it has in common with the original product is the logo. The bogan looked at Gretchen quizzically, wondering whether she was having trouble reading the English alphabet.

Meanwhile, Foster's and Lion Nathan were laughing all the way to the bank. European beers were generally sold in 330 ml bottles instead of the Aussie standard 375 ml. This effectively meant that they'd moved from selling 375 ml slabs of locally made beer for $35 to selling 330 ml slabs of locally made beer for $45. The licence fees only took up a small slice of this massive bogan windfall. But the new bogan is blissfully happy. He is now a man of the world, even when not wearing his Bintang singlet.

'Fuck off, we're full' stickers

The bogan loves its car, and the bogan loves putting bumper stickers on its car. A sentiment that has been distilled into a few

short words appeals to the bogan's belief that the universal order is fundamentally simple to grasp, which is convenient since its past experiences of thinking about things too hard have proven frustrating and ultimately unrewarding. Perhaps this explains why the bogan can sustain the conviction that Australia's landmass of 7,682,300 square kilometres cannot physically accommodate any more than its current population of just over 22 million people.

This idea is perplexing, but the bogan appears to believe it firmly enough to plaster it on the back of its beloved car. Believing Australia is fatally overcrowded, one does wonder why the bogan pumped out three kids in the last two and half years, and this is yet another example of the kind of fascinating contradictions constantly thrown up by the phenomenon of boganism.

At the risk of doing TBL readers' work for them, the sticker makes a lot more sense when you look at it this way: Australia is not 'full' as far as the bogan's own kind is concerned – the message is intended for foreign immigrants, particularly asylum seekers. The bogan is not racist, but believes that immigrants (only the brown ones, of course) don't 'assimilate', by which it means they don't become bogans. Naturally, the bogan has never actually met a refugee before, and bases this opinion solely on something Aaron was saying in between mouthfuls of beef and black bean the other night. One of the most illustrative insights into the bogan's confounding pathology is that the bogan claims to like each and every brown person it has ever chanced to meet, yet continues to maintain the opinion that every single other brown person is some kind of hybrid of Osama Bin Laden and Idi Amin.

To its marginal credit, and despite the fact that the bogan drives about with a racist statement on the back of its car, a true bogan is unlikely to be a member of an active white supremacist hate group. That would mean straying too far outside of the warm, cradling mainstream and, besides, their meetings clash with *Two and a Half Men*. Also to its credit is the accurate grammar and syntax of the printed sentiment. No, the 'Fuck off, we're full' sticker is racism-as-automotive adornment, a nod and a wink to other racist bogans – 'Yes, I'm a racist too, it's okay, you belong. Now please admire my sick rims.'

Thailand

The recent proliferation of discount airfares has seen the rise of the wise, well-travelled bogan. Five years ago, Bali was the best place to observe herds of shirtless, migratory bogans in the wild, but the rise of terrorism in Indonesia, Schapelle Corby's well-publicised failure as an importer/exporter, and the entry of Jetstar into the Australia–Thailand route has seen a new habitat emerge. Motivated by the lure of cheap alcohol, spicy food (ordered 'mild'), and sexploitation, the bogan has embraced Bangkok, Phuket, and that full moon place as its modern spiritual retreat.

Thailand is close enough for the bogan to leave its nest at dawn, read the latest movie readapted to a novel, or watch *Anchorman*, and land in time to be slurping from a bucket by evening. Much like the Contiki tour, Thailand allows the bogan to believe it is having an exotic cultural experience while speaking English, interacting only with other bogans (hopefully including attractive British and Scandinavian bogans) and engaging in activities they engage in at home.

Safely ensconced in a Phuket tourist resort or an Australian themed bar, the bogan can drink near toxic amounts of cheap beer, get bronzed, eat spring rolls, adorn itself with braids, tramp stamps or tribal tattoos, and watch *Anchorman* again. The more adventurous bogan can have its photo taken sitting on an elephant or in front of a temple, or posing shirtless and sunburnt on a generic beach.

At the end of the week, the bogan can round out its travel experience with its fourth visit to the Khao San Road tourist pit, where it can interact with impoverished locals for the purpose of methodically screwing them out of $1.30 of the $1.40 profit margin in their fake sunglasses' starting price. Invariably, one of the items purchased is a beer singlet for itself or a loved one to wear at the gym back home. Other items regularly witnessed by Jetstar cabin crew include Buddhist iconography, stolen bar mat(s), painfully idealistic (and often misspelled or erroneously translated) tattoos in the local language, bogus high fashion brands, and a new-found capacity for credible racism.

Once home, the bogan will get mild Thai food delivered to their next house party, enthusiastically regaling attendees with its bucket guzzling exploits through a mouthful of Pad Thai. The worldly bogan will employ its one word Thai vocabulary to attempt to say thank you to the food delivery guy, even though he's an engineering student from Delhi.

M.I.A.'s 'Paper Planes'

Mathangi Arulpragasam is a 34-year-old woman of Tamil origin, who spent nine of her first eleven years in Sri Lanka and Southern India on the run because her father was involved in Tamil militancy and civil war. In 1986, she arrived in England as a refugee alongside her mother and brother, and Mathangi learned English while living on a council estate in South London. Bogans would not approve of this story.

Whether it's beating them up at train stations, running out of their taxis without paying, or just general derision, there is a significant number of bogans who simply do not like 'curries'. It believes that curries smell bad, want to steal its job, and listen to stupid high-pitched music that isn't their own stupid, high-pitched music. When the white bogan is in the club, it would rather be surrounded by other white bogans and listen to sick songs like M.I.A.'s 'Paper Planes'.

As evidenced in the video, the bogan appeal of the song is clear. While the repetitive melody and lyrics make things easier for the bogan when it is on the dance floor, by far the most important thing that 'Paper Planes' provides the bogan is the chance to shape its hand into a pistol of some sort and pretend that it is firing a gun. And not just once or twice, but the bogan can fire its imaginary gun *48 times* during the song. This appeals to the bogan's desire to feel close to *Underbelly*. Now that it's firing its gun 48 times in the club, it is more like *Underbelly* than ever before. The bogan feels empowered, dangerous and desirable.

With its focus exclusively on waiting for the next chorus – and certainly with no intention of listening to anything else M.I.A. ever recorded – the bogan's attention strays during the parts in between. The bogan does not realise that during this time Mathangi Arulpragasam's lyrics include phrases such as 'third world democracy', and that Arulpragasam's music is highly political. To quote the lady herself, the song is 'about people driving taxicabs all day and living in a shitty apartment and "appearing" really threatening to society. But not being so . . . I wanted to see if I could write songs about something important and make it sound like nothing. And it kind of worked.' Indeed, the bogan is utterly oblivious that it is being entertained by an activist curry refugee.

A group of bogans later exit the club, feeling strangely energised from their dozen Jagerbombs each, and also from animatedly discharging their dance-floor weapons 48 times in the space of three and a half minutes. They need an outlet. Up ahead, they spy an Indian student who appears to be carrying a laptop bag . . .

Border Security: Australia's Front Line

The bogan is not racist. It is, however, very much not in favour of crime and criminals, unless they are nicking street signs and bar mats, or exporting illicit substances into Indonesia, which, after all, are harmless pastimes. People *importing* illicit substances into Australia, on the other hand, are despicable scum – this perception being reinforced by our very own prime minister. Is it the bogan's fault that these uniquely disgusting criminals are from another country? Obviously *not*.

Channel 7, realising the awesome spending power of the bogan, the awesome cost-saving power of reality TV, and the awesome bogan love of catching (foreign) criminals, combined them all in the greatest bogan program of all time: *Border Security: Australia's Front Line*. After all, even though the bogan is not racist, what better way to catch these abominable criminals than to whack a camera or two in a large room replete with suspicious-looking foreigners?

Despite the fact that the customs queues at Australia's major airports are overwhelmingly full of white, returning Australians, tired and emotional about having to wait in a queue in order to be told to pay GST on the watch they bought in Switzerland, the bulk of *Border Security: Australia's Front Line* is entirely devoted to filming shifty looking visitors from South East Asia or the Middle East having their loot of rice and sardines rifled through.

Even better than this, the show is portentously narrated by Grant Bowler, who most bogans remember as playing Constable Wayne Patterson in *Blue Heelers*: Mt Thomas' Front Line, where he was living the bogan dream by engaging in PG-rated heavy petting with Lisa McCune.

Settled in its interest-free lounge suite, the bogan is able to vicariously enjoy the act of keeping Australia safe from people it steadfastly refuses to understand. Its endorphins gush on each and every occasion that such a person is not able to move about in the manner that they hope to. At the completion of the show, the bogan is reassured that it has done its part to defend the nation that it has done so very little to create.

Ernie Dingo

As we have amply discussed here, the bogan is fiercely proud to be Australian. It is wracked with patriotic quiverings whenever Australia's history is mentioned. It is like the proverbial horny bull at a rusty gate when making a spectacle of its 'patriotism' – whether on its car or on its skin. It fully supports any initiative to keep the country's borders safe from outsiders. The bogan wants foreigners to know that Australia is bogan country, and any prospective Australian should become a bogan themselves if they expect to be welcomed – otherwise, they should simply 'go home'.

The bogan believes it possesses all qualities unique to Australians, and has appointed itself both gatekeeper and keymaster to the thrice-bolted security locker of boganic Australianness. The existence of indigenous Australians, however, throws a distinctly obstinate spanner into the works of this line of thinking. Whenever a bogan uses the apparently watertight 'I was here first' logic to engender in itself a snugly fitting sense of unchallenged entitlement to the country, a distant but unshakeable feeling of self-doubt is stimulated. When this feeling gets too much for the bogan, it reminds itself that it likes Ernie Dingo.

Like many Aboriginal people who are elite athletes or media personalities, Ernie Dingo is embraced with enthusiasm by bogans as the smiley, clean-cut face of Aboriginal Australia. In his TV journeys into the outback, Ernie allows the bogan to see the country it is so proud of, witness some maxtreme four wheel driving and perhaps a spot of fishing. It desirously gazes at sumptuous food and luxury accommodation, and chuckles at the assorted on-road hijinks, all without, of course, having to leave the couch. More comforting still for the bogan, engagement with the local population is kept to a minimum, and when it does occur, it is at the depth one might expect to accidentally plumb while on a Contiki tour of Thailand.

The bogan's take on the situation is similar to the bogan's take on most politically charged topics – simplistic and ill-informed, yet held on to with the white-knuckled grip of the truly terrified. When quizzed on Aboriginal disadvantage, the bogan will take a massive swig on its sixth massive can of Woodstock and tell you everything would be perfectly fine for Indigenous Australians if they only 'got off the booze'. It will tell you Aboriginals get more than their share of government handouts, while itself remaining vigilant for opportunities to rort workers' compensation schemes, and it vociferously decries any attempt to reduce Indigenous poverty or increase lifespans as 'political correctness gone mad'. The bogan is, however, happy to be pro-Aboriginal when it comes to Ernie Dingo, who delivers it sharp pangs of patriotic pride mixed with pleasant, light-hearted, unchallenging entertainment, just as the bogan is happy to take ownership of any Indigenous athlete who earns a gold medal or premiership trophy. The bogan does a similar thing with New Zealand actors and, at times, homosexuals of note, but is quick to switch around when they fall out of favour, and toss them on the scrapheap of fame.

Hot Asian chicks

There are hundreds of thousands of white bogan males in Australia, and they know many things. They know that Australia is the best country in the world. They know that Asia is only good for Phuket, Foakleys, and maxing out at the Full Moon Party. They know that they like their women looking like Katie Price. They know that immigrants should get out and stop taking their jobs. But, paradoxically, they also know that hot Asian chicks are . . . hot.

The bogan covetousness of the hot Asian chick is proof that the white bogan male is actually a great bloke – lighthouse of cosmopolitanism and compassion that shines across the hostile seas. If the illegal fishing boats full of Afghani immigrants that wash up on Ashmore Reef actually were full of hot Asian chicks, you can be absolutely certain that the bogan would not have railroaded the federal government into declaring a six-month suspension on processing asylum seeker claims. Indeed, if word got out that these boats were laden with the finest treasures of the orient, hordes of bogans would be strapping long range fuel tanks and floral bouquets onto their jet skis, and trying to intercept the vessels themselves. Nobody would be watching *Border Security* on the plasma any longer; the entire male audience would be out trying to harness Australia onto a boat trailer and drag it closer to Java with the help of over 10,000 fluorescent Falcon XR8s.

Unfortunately for the male cosmo-bogue, the concentration of hot Asian chicks on these boats is not as high as it wishes. As such, the bogan keeps its covetousness of them entirely separate from its views on immigration, saving it and its friends from having to sit down and synchronise any dissonant information. This leaves the bogan with the time to go out and get max plastered. Out at the drinking barn, the bogan collective will make loud comments early in the evening about how the Asian guy a few metres away is certainly not well endowed. As the night wears on, the attention shifts back to the other gender, and when an attractive Asian female is sighted at the other end of the bar, a bogan will invariably announce to his friends that he's 'going to be eating Chinese tonight' to roaring approval.

The bogan confidently eyes the Asian chick. It has witnessed hours of them copping it on the net, and has a thorough knowledge of how they are seduced. Purchasing a house chardonnay, it approaches the female, who is already sipping on her cocktail. 'Here, sweetheart, how about you have a drink of this, and then we'll go back to my bedroom so that you can discover Australia?' The girl observes the bogan with an exotic blend of horror and amusement, and walks off. Reporting back to its mates, the bogan explains that 'she wasn't hot, so I told her to get out of Australia'. The night ends with the spurned bogan performing the Stranger on itself in its computer chair, to the familiar scenes of *Asian Slutmax Volume Four*.

New Zealand

Confused and threatened that bogan deities David Boon, Ricky Ponting and Princess Mary are Tasmanians, the bogan needed a new place to belittle. Casting its eye further out to sea, Jetstar found the bogan a new target, one rich with a range of celebrities to poach, new ways for the bogan to recycle old jokes about incest, accents or bestiality, and nicer scenery. Essentially what insular middle-class America uses Canada for.

Because the bogan believes that Australia is totally unique, it finds itself under great pressure to differentiate its nation from the nation most similar to it. It will mainly just emphasise New Zealand's abundance of sheep (35 million, compared to Australia's 80 million). Once this myth is debunked, the bogan has very little to say, aside from recounting another joke about sex with sheep to comfort itself back into its default stupor. Minutes later, long after the conversation has changed tack, the bogan will curse itself for not making a Hobbit joke. And then make it anyway.

By preserving in its mind its notion of New Zealand, the nation, the bogan attains someone to look down upon, and a way to preserve its thin veneer of national identity. Whenever the bogan discovers that a successful person is a Kiwi, they will selectively vow that they're actually adopted Australians. Talented examples of this include Russell Crowe, Crowded House, Xena and Evermore. Talentless polymer husk examples of this include Richard Wilkins. Importantly for the bogan's sense of financial power, New Zealand is one of the few English-speaking countries where the Australian dollar will buy more than one unit of the local currency. As it disembarks its Jetstar flight in Christchurch, this financial transaction makes the bogan instantly 25% more energised. After a lifetime of eliciting laughter and approval whenever it asked for 'fush and chups' on the east coast of Australia, the bogan mind is unable to fathom why the tattooed guy in the Christchurch takeaway store looks like he's soon to glass the bogan. At this point, the bogan troupe scuttles out of the store, strangers in a strange land.

But the bogan isn't in Christchurch to scout for new jokes or new musical talent to kidnap, for its music needs are exclusively spoon-fed to it by commercial radio or the Hottest 100 on Australia Day. No, the bogan is in Christchurch to be maxtreme. While 90% of the bogan's thought time about New Zealand involves sheep jokes, the remaining 10% involves loudly vowing to do intense ski and bungy jumping in Queenstown. The seven-day trip will involve nightly Queenstown drinking binges, during which the bogan will complain that Kiwi piss isn't as good as Australian piss (while failing to recognise that 90% of the white wine they drink at home is Kiwi), before lining up to order four more, and boasting about how they were 'only like two Aussie bucks each! 'On its way back to its hotel, it will tell its travel companions Maori jokes (directly adapted from Aboriginal jokes) in hushed tones, terrified that the All Blacks will appear and beat the shit out of it.

MUSIC
AND
NIGHTLIFE

Ruining music festivals

A new type of festival goer has emerged in recent years. First observed around the turn of the millennium at the Melbourne Big Day Out, it goes just to say it did, and because everyone else does. It pays hundreds of dollars to attend festivals, often forking out top dollar to scalpers at the last minute after its lack of organisational and budgeting skills prevent it from acquiring tickets in advance.

It attends festivals only to spend the vast majority of its time hovering around the beer garden in a valiant attempt to avoid actually seeing any bands. This is because it does not in fact know any of the bands playing, not having heard them on commercial radio or seen them on *Video Hits*. (There is one rare exception – when there is a DJ tent, or famous electronic artist performing. In this instance, it instantly congregates with its kind, pops candy, and proceeds to beat the crap out of its peers in sheer happiness at the glowing solidarity provided by Girl Talk's 'Shut the Club Down').

As the day goes on and it consumes far more alcohol and drugs than it can possibly handle, it begins to get agitated. It has strayed too far from its natural habitat. There are too many emos around. Everyone is wearing black, and Travisty t-shirts are few and far between. It gravitates towards others like it, easily identifiable by lack of a shirt, intense sunburn, an Australian flag draped over their shoulders, a Southern Cross tattoo, or all of the above.

Once a group of sufficient size is formed, confidence begins to swell among the herd. It, with the security of its new posse, can now begin hurling insults towards emos, who are identifiable to the herd by their lack of Travisty attire. The herd, the alcohol and the drugs have given it super powers, and it uses those powers for the most worthy cause it can think of: to intimidate foreign-looking people into kissing the Australian flag.

The proliferation of the festival-going, shirtless, sunburnt, Australian flag draped, Southern Cross tattoo bearing bogan has ruined many a festival. In fact, the bogan has the unique ability to ruin any public event or place, including the Melbourne Cup, one-day cricket, Cronulla Beach, your favourite bar, New Year's Eve, and Christmas.

Cover bands

Bogans love commercial radio. But, with the limiting nature of only liking five different artists (selected arbitrarily from P!nk, Snow Patrol, U2, AC/DC, Nickelback, Coldplay, Green Day or any remix of anything), the bogan can quickly grow bored. Commercial radio does what it can, by playing these artists on constant rotation, but still there is a void, particularly when it comes to live music. P!nk's constant defilement of major arenas notwithstanding, major international acts rarely venture to the antipodes.

Enter the cover band. You know them. They were the guys who formed a band in Year 9, playing gigs at lunch to 30 kids who then got booted out of the auditorium for crowd surfing. That was, until the point they formed a cover band, the highpoint of their lives. It's Darren, Sam and Clint, plus Clint's younger brother who they recruited to play bass because their old bass player's wife won't let him out on weeknights/their old bass player got hooked on ice and disappeared in Darwin/they never see their bass player anymore. And, in a desperate attempt to reclaim the euphoria that is live performance, they go to the same pub, on the same night, every week, and play the same songs. To the same bogans.

And bogans love it. Having only five artists to listen to means that opportunities for attending live rock performances (is there another kind?) are few and far between. Sport notwithstanding, communal entertainment is usually designated as being for 'other people'. Opera ('poofs'), dance ('poofs'), non-rock music ('poofs'), comedy ('Is it Hughesy? No? Poofs.') and the theatre ('poofs') are all for a cultural subset that is not bogan, leaving only whichever *Fast and the Furious* film is in cinemas, or the pub with a cover band. Those five artists mentioned above can be re-created without the talent, verve or creativity of their original members but, importantly, the cover band will mimic each song down to the 16th beat.

Thus, the bogans can bounce around, singing only to the chorus of 'Betterman' and 'Jessie's Girl', while screaming for post-Californication Chili Peppers, and feel inordinately cultured. Meanwhile the boys from 'Jet Black' or 'Crazygarden' reel out 'hit after hit', while the bogan hopes no one notices when it jumps into the loud bit from 'Blister in the Sun' one measure too soon.

Commercial radio

PBS, RRR and other community stations the nation over are the enemy of the bogan. While the hipster is obsessed with finding music that the rest of the world is blissfully unaware of, the bogan approaches its radio from a different perspective. They treat radio as a filter, something that can take music they already like (Bon Jovi, Nickelback, Snow Patrol et al), process it, and find new music that is *identical to it in almost every way*.

But for the bogan, this is not enough. It is never enough. They grow weary of hearing 'Chasing Cars' again and again, so someone needs to remix it. Suddenly, Starsailor's 'Four to the Floor' has a bitchin' dance-floor mix and takes over the airwaves, and bogans are happy. For a while. Then, Eric Prydz (or Prydg, or Prizjch) decides to take an eighties camp classic . . . and remix it. The bogan likes this greatly, because it can imagine, while listening to Nova, the film clip, with its ample bouncing bosoms.

During daylight hours, when nonstop remixes or replays may seem inappropriate, commercial radio knows that not even the bogan can handle Coldplay *ad nauseum*. They bring in 'comedians' to make prank phone calls. All day. With remixed music playing in the background. Bogans can then engage in one of their favourite pastimes: standing around at work/uni/TAFE attempting to recreate the entire prank phone call verbatim. With a stunning lack of success.

Conversely, if a commercial radio station cannot afford the appropriate 'comedians', they bring in 'celebrities' to abuse people, in a pale imitation of the genuine hatred of life and people of AM radio. This appeals to another of the bogan's chief loves: confected outrage. The bogan can then feel wonderful by hating the very person they tune in to listen to every day.

On commercial AM radio, to which bogans tune in once they turn 39, the announcers allow them to engage in the number one pastime of middle-aged bogans everywhere: yelling at the radio. However, unlike FM radio, where the bogan will yell at Kyle Sandilands for being Kyle Sandilands without changing station, on AM radio, the announcer will carefully pick a topic that he (it's almost always he) knows will result in an orgiastic, national, simultaneous bout of bogan rage – banning burqas is always an excellent option – and opine that these foreigners have no right to do whatever it is that they do that makes bogans uncomfortable.

Yet the bogan, young and old, remains dissatisfied. Something is missing. The love of commercial radio can only go so far in creating a unique identity for the bogan, and the bogan has a biological imperative to colonise things other people enjoy. Thus, they discovered Triple J, much like white people discovered Australia, then began to beat the shit out of the locals. The first warning signs came a decade ago, when 'Pretty Fly for a White Guy' topped the Hottest 100. But the signs were ignored. These interlopers would leave if Triple J introduced Aussie hip-hop to its rotation, surely? No, because the bogan is cunning, and can adapt. 'Nosebleed Section' thus found itself in Triple J Hottest 100 *of all time*.

All of this brings us to the natural evolutionary musical endgame: Kings of Leon . . .

Kings of Leon

Kings of Leon have consciously adapted themselves into the bogan meta-band. They tick every conceivable bogan pleasure box. Sometime between their second and third albums, Kings of Leon realised that there is a clear correlation between the number of records a band sells and the similarity of their sound to U2's. They also sing about sex, without metaphor or innuendo, which removes the need to interpret lyrics and still titillates the bogan.

They emerged, fully formed, from the world of indie-rock critical adoration, with songs like 'Sex on Fire'. This gave the bogan a song with a main hook featuring a lyric containing the words 'yeah!' and 'sex!'. Words that the bogan could then sing along to loudly as their local cover band played that now-ubiquitous paean to herpes. Bogans like rooting stuff, they like burning stuff, they like exclamation marks, and they like mindless affirmation. 'YEEEEEEEEEEEEHAAAAAH, THIS SEX IS ON FIRE!!!' is a scientifically blended formula, a tripod of bogan trigger points. There was no conceivable way that such a song would not endear itself to the bogan.

Moreover, they sing repeatedly about having sex with groupies. Male bogans will thus dream of having sex with underaged, worshipful girls, while female bogans will dream of being said sexual supplicants. The band being ruggedly handsome southern-rock types who regularly visit the antipodes, female bogans can positively taste the back sweat, and flock to see them, listen to them and generally think a lot about them.

Commercial radio rapidly realised this, and began looping Kings of Leon to play at least twice every half-hour, and incorporating Kings of Leon into every conceivable competition they ran. Of course, KoL could be painted coconuts playing speed calypso funk, and the bogan would love them just the same, provided the radio networks played them 10–15 times a day, the ad with their song was on air all day, every day, and you could win a night with them in Vegas if you bought enough cans of Mother, etc.

It was, and presently remains, a match made in bogan heaven.

Ministry of Sound

While the bogan can't always decide whether its favourite country is Bali or Phuket, it knows that come Sundays, its favourite techno band is Ministry of Sound. Just like commercial radio, the Ministry of Sound corporation acts as a filter for the bogan, packaging the world of music into glamorously branded compilations so that it doesn't need to think, search or be faced with the confusion of choice. The full spectrum of the bogan's moods can thus be catered to by MoS compilations like *Maximum Bass Overdrive* (fighty), *Clubbers Guide* (fighty/strutty), *Chillout Sessions* (fighty/strung out), and the *MoS Annual* (fighty/nostalgic).

While the bogan is unaware of the origins of Ministry of Sound, it knows it's something to do with Ibiza in the Greek Islands, which is probably full of hot sluts. If a song is too slow for the club, the bogan knows that Ministry can be relied upon to staple a programmed kick drum and a pneumatic buzzing synth sound to it. If a song is too frenetic for a Sunday afternoon, the bogan knows that Ministry agrees, has removed the kick drum, and called in some chick who sounds like Enya to sigh over a sample of breaking waves and wind chimes. The bogan is safe from harm in its ministerial cocoon.

By fencing off the galaxy of music into a small pen, Ministry of Sound also enables the bogan to confidently participate in conversations about dance, electronica and ambient music with its friends. Even better, the range of MoS branded apparel allows the bogan to physically affiliate itself with the logo, and then strut around like a DJ/celebrity. The male bogan knows full well that an uptempo Ministry compilation is the correct mating call to pair with its plumage of large biceps and personalised numberplates while it competes for turf up and down popular nightclub strips.

Many a new bogan has heard the urban legend about the time that a bogan was in a metal club for its cousin's birthday, unhappy with the confusing music that it didn't know how to dance to. It approached the DJ booth, demanding that the DJ play some 'fucking Ministry or something good'. Unexpectedly, the DJ nodded enthusiastically and started playing an industrial metal song called 'Jesus Built My Hotrod'. Few modern bogans have yet realised what went wrong, but many now cautiously add the '. . . of Sound' suffix to their request, just in case.

Indie rock choruses

'Indie rock?' I hear you ask. 'Surely not!' But alas, the bogan, or at least a small subset of boganity – the same subset that brings Kings of Leon to the top of the Hottest 100, no doubt – are broadening their musical reach. These trendsetting bogans are on a mission, a mission to appear cool to bogans everywhere by unveiling to those bogans new music that has been publicly available for at least six months.

At the time of this book's publication, these bogans will be seeking out, say, LCD Soundsystem, or perhaps Vampire Weekend. They will regale their less enlightened compatriots with the sheer awesomeness of this new band that has four full-length albums and countless production credits. To build their credibility beyond all doubt, they will attend the gig when the band comes out over summer. And they will sing along heartily. But only to the choruses.

The bogan, lacking sufficient attention span, or genuine desire, to listen to a song more than five times, will decide that it will suffice to learn the words to the chorus or main hook of the band's lead single, and rehearse a rousing rendition. This rendition will be offered, pro bono, to other fans at the band's gig. Come the first line of the second verse of 'One Crowded Hour', however, the bogan trails off in a pool of mumbling incoherence. Bored now with the verse-y bits it does not know, it turns to its less-cool friend it brought and begins a conversation about how wasted it is, with little regard for those who may enjoy the verse-y bits.

When the band has exhausted the three songs Triple J has played, the bogan's boredom reaches the threshold where going to the bar is the only option. In its clueless and blustering shove-through to the bar, the bogan bumps into some hapless hipster who's busy trying to look as if he's only there because he was on the door. The hipster drops his Leffe Blonde, and tries to look annoyed, bored and non-threatening at the same time. Unfortunately, he cannot avoid rolling his eyes, and that's enough for the bogan, who takes a swing and is consequently turfed out by security and barred for life. By morning, this story has transformed itself into an epic tale wherein the bogan took on five Maori security guards and won, then went home with a corporate lawyer-cum-lingerie model. Oh, after he saw an awesome, cred-inducing gig of indie rock.

Your favourite bar

The non-bogan probably thinks its favourite bar is too well hidden, too small and contains too many bearded patrons to ever appear on the bogan's colonisation radar. An oasis of reason amid an ever-expanding desert of bogan-inflicted chaos, the non-bogan's favourite bar is one of the few remaining places with immunity to the boganic plague. Run by an owner-operator, it might host some low-key live tunes, and is probably even within walking distance of hipster residential enclaves. There is no dress code. There are no commercial remixes. And no one ever tries to start glassing fights. It's never too full. There is no 'list'. And there is never a line-up to get in.

But be warned: the bogan is coming. Once content with mass glassings and gropings to a Top 40 remix soundtrack at high capacity beer barns located on major arterial roads and shopping strips, the bogan now has an inkling that it is missing out on something. Like a child coveting the toy that the other kid has because the other kid has it, the bogan wants to take the non-bogan's favourite bar from them not because it really wants it, but because it doesn't want them to have something it hasn't got.

The bogan will learn of the non-bogan's favourite bar when the trashmedia report that an actor from *Underbelly* went there once. Like a moth to a computer screen in a dark room, the bogan will not be able to. When the invasion begins, the non-bogan will at first passively resist. 'If I just ignore them, they'll have no reason to bother me, and they will soon realise that it's not their scene,' the non-bogan might think to itself.

But things will soon begin to change. Despite the bar's stunning variety of local and imported beers, Corona and Beck's will dominate sales, along with any kind of explosive beverage. Orange-skinned femme-bogues will start dancing in the middle of the place, even though there is no dance floor and it's never really been a place where people dance. They will then get bored and complain loudly that they've 'never heard this song before. Play some Kings of Leon!' Drinks will cost more after bashings and glassings see the bar attain 'high-risk' status leading to higher liquor licensing fees, and bogans are willing to pay more for far inferior drinks. Finally, the non-bogan's favourite bar will be purchased by a football player, or Woolworths, and turned into a pizza bar.

Game over.

PSYCHOLOGICAL PROFILE

Political correctness gone mad

Possibly the most abused phrase in our contemporary lexicon, 'political correctness', initially referred to the project of re-engineering certain terms to remove implicit discrimination and promote neutrality and inclusiveness in language. For instance, proponents of political correctness advocate the use of the utilitarian 'flight attendant', 'chairperson' and 'thyroid challenged Australian' over more charged terms like 'stewardess', 'chairman' and 'Joe Hockey' (sorry Joe – easy target). Uncomfortable with the threat this posed to their perceived right to insult people they don't care about, the term was seized on by right-wing commentators and redeployed as a catch-all pejorative phrase to deride the entire spectrum of progressive thought. They won, and over the years, the addendum 'gone mad' emerged, asserting that, much like Ken Bruce, political correctness had gone batshit crazy and become a slavering, rabid, totalitarian Soviet bear, hurtling towards the horizon, wild-eyed and hungry, looking to devour our Freedom and Way Of Life.

The bogan latched onto this concept less than a year ago and, ignorant of the term's troubled etymology, has since been arming itself with the phrase in any discussion of political or social issues, in the time-honoured bogan fashion of getting these kinds of things wrong. Spurred on by the reactionary commentators most directly responsible for its sorely uninformed yet nonetheless adamantly held opinion on everything from immigration policy to juvenile justice, the bogan now uses the phrase to stand in place of any actual analysis, the exact adult equivalent of shoving Duplo in its ears and shouting 'Do not want.'

Because the bogan's political convictions are formed entirely out of received wisdom, the argumentative shorthand of 'political correctness gone mad' and similar slogans is of great use to the bogan. The key appeal lies in not having to interrupt its routine of consumption to attain the wide reading of history and current affairs needed for making an informed comment. Further, being able to so succinctly write off anything exhibiting tolerance and compassion towards people different to itself allows the bogan to effectively reinforce a conviction of its sole entitlement to that cocoon of suburban orthodoxy that provides such utility for crypto-fascist politicians and marketers of energy drinks.

Going to work in the mines

The young bogan male craves adventure and violence. Although the military offers the opportunity to undertake this without the threat of arrest, the bogan finds the threat of death far less palatable. As a result, it is significantly more common to loudly profess a desire to join the army than to actually join it. Instead, the bogan can get his adventure in Western Australia, forgoing the chance to kill things for the chance to dig a big hole and earn a stupid amount of money.

He isn't actually going off to war, but the bogan's family and friends will treat his departure in a similar solemn ceremonial way. While in a remote area of Western Australia, the bogan will ply his modest skill set, be it at boilermaking, engineering, food preparation, or holding a traffic signpost, earning in excess of $500 a day. This financial windfall opens the glittering door to hyper-bogan consumption. Within months, he is playing GTA on his new 125-inch full HD, 3D, LED TV, ripping doughnuts in his shiny Chevrolet ute and drinking phenomenal amounts of locally brewed Stella Artois.

His roster allows him a few consecutive days off each month, which he uses to fly down to Perth with his new mining buddies. They're there for a good time, not a long time, and the wallets are bulging. They saunter with an aura of invincibility that can only be derived from waging war on the frontier, though in this case the adversary is a pristine natural environment. At the poker tables at Burswood casino, they gamble beyond the realm of any sense. The local card sharks generally pocket thousands of mining dollars thanks to their superior card playing skills, making the bogan squadron irritable. Eventually they retreat to the strippers to tuck $50 notes into garter belts and drink more Stella.

After a couple of years of this, the bogan returns home from war to a hero's welcome. He is tanned, he has more Christian Audigier products than anyone in his suburb, and there is a jet ski trailer hitched to the back of the Chevrolet. Soon, though, the money runs out. His one-man commodity boom is over. The reality of a normal income level quickly kicks in. He can't afford to go to the casino so often, the strippers have stopped treating him like a celebrity and a new model of ute has been released that he's unable to get finance for. Bitter with the world, he contents himself with cutting off people when merging lanes, calling pedestrians poofs, and thinking back to the time when he was king.

New Year's resolutions

In a rare display of patience, the bogan has resisted temptation and waited all year. And when, on January first, it wakes up with fireworks and the familiar clink of Jagerbombs still ringing in its ears, it is ready to act. The bogan vows that this year will be different. This will be the year that it shows 'them'. That afternoon it compiles a lengthy list of goals, revelling in the sense of occasion that the first day of the year grants to such a list. It vows to become fitter, happier, more productive, more spiritual, more maxtreme.

On 2 January the bogan digs out its pair of sports shorts and marches off to Fitness First to sign up for 12 months. On 3 January it enrols in a short course that will provide it with the singing skills to dominate *Australian Idol*. On 4 January it buys the leather-bound tome that will house its family tree project. On 5 January it attends the gym. On 6 January it is virtually immobile due to the volume of bicep curls it insisted on doing. On 11 January it returns to the gym, somewhat humbled, and increasingly aware that getting either huge or svelte will take quite some time.

A month later, its sports shorts are back in the drawer, buried under the sedimentary layer of its bourbon-stained Southern Cross Australia Day attire. The first six hours of the singing course failed to transform it into a pop idol, so it blamed the teacher for being useless and discontinued its attendance. One way in which it had become more like a pop idol, however, came via its lack of gym attendance in over three weeks. The bogan's physique was closer to Susan Boyle's than it had ever been. The only family tree project that was underway in the McMansion was the female bogan nagging its spouse to take the baubles off the dead pine limb in the rumpus room and cart it out to the nature strip so it could become someone else's problem. Not an ideal outcome, but the bogan knows that it must wait until 1 January the following year before it can ponder new targets.

News Limited

There is nothing a bogan loves more than being outraged. The bogan is most fond of being outraged at people who, for a variety of reasons, it has made minimal effort to understand, especially on ethnic, national, or religious grounds. And there is no better bowser of fury-inducing rocket fuel than News Ltd's very own line of Australian newspapers. The only rumoured greater source is whatever is written at the bottom of a glass of Bundaberg and Coke.

With an array of columnists with a hard-wired awareness of the bogan's panic buttons, the topic *du jour* on the comments page (and, increasingly, the papers' website blogs) invariably revolves around finding scapegoats for bad things. Often, those at fault for the world's malaise are the very people who are the victims of it. Thus stimulated, bogans are equipped with sufficient righteous indignation to cover any encounter with a fellow at the water cooler, foodcourt, playgroup or other designated daytime bogan convergence point. Once discussion of last night's episode of *Master Chef* and *Border Security* is exhausted, that is. This discussion tends to follow similar themes to the commentary printed in that morning's tabloids. Indeed, many a bogan has been caught repeating a slightly more obscure columnist verbatim, in an effort to pass off the opinion as their own. Example:

Bogan 1: 'Can you believe they're actually going through with an emissions trading thingy because of climate change? I mean, for all intensive purposes, Australia doesn't mean anything to climate change!'

Bogan 2: 'Tell me about it – it's all a crock anyway . . . there's a whole bunch of scientists – like 100,000 – who say it's all bull, and that climate change is a myth made up to charge us higher taxes so we can give Abos more welfare that they'll spend on booze! And I reckon this is a perfect opportunity for the Liberals to make a case for the next election – there's a silent majority out there that's waiting for a party to push this whole thing to one side, but the lefty media won't publish anything. It's Political Correctness Gone Mad!'

Bogan 1: 'That's funny, I read *exactly* the same thing in Andrew Bolt's column this morning . . .'

Bogan 2: 'Really? Oh well . . . what a coincidence . . . ha ha . . . Great minds think alike!'

Of course, this is not limited only to News Ltd's Victorian or Novocastrian endeavours. The *Courier-Mail*, the *NT News*, the *Adelaide Advertiser* and, of course, the incredible www.news. com.au (news being in the title makes it easily googlable without actually knowing any news websites – ideal for the thick-of-skull) are all bastions of bogan confected outrage. Enough outrage to tide the bogan through to 6:30 pm, on its choice of Channel 7 or 9.

N.B. The bogan would enjoy *The Australian* too, but its worrisome habit of using too many confusing phrases like 'leftist agenda' makes it unsuitable reading for the bogan.

Late night logistics

Usually the bogan just doesn't care. Its conduct is that of a self-interested cretin, utterly unwilling to think sequentially, and merrily taking delight in the misfortune of others. But like an octogenarian who has exhausted his supply of Viagra, there is a definite soft spot in the bogan's leathery shell. This hidden side of the bogan is a compassionate one, it is a supportive one, it is a thoughtful one. The bogan wants nothing but the best for you.

Unfortunately, the bogan suffers from confidence issues, and usually finds itself too shy to express its beautiful true self to strangers. This is society's loss, and it pains the bogan to the point that it will turn to hard liquor to dull the persistent pangs of guilt and shame. You can find the bogan standing in a dark corner of a bar late in the evening, intoxicated on its own existential torment, and hoping that one more drink will liberate it from its inhibitions.

Over in the middle of the bar is an obnoxious drunkard who is rigorously exercising its freedom of speech. The drunkard is gesticulating wildly to make its fallacious points, with its tentacles flinging dangerously close to bystanders. Mid-sentence, its motor skills finally abandon it, causing its bottle of locally brewed, foreign label beer to fly from its hand. Time stops. Or it goes into that bullet time thing from *The Matrix*.

The camera pans to the unfulfilled bogan in the corner, watching the bottle majestically soaring towards the wall. Caught in the moment, the bogan forgets its fears. The bogan is suddenly alive, catlike, purposeful. As the bottle crushes into the plaster, the bogan is moving towards the drunkard, ready to offer advice and assistance. A temporary flash of self-doubt returns, so it rehearses its proposed dialogue.

'Excuse me, sir, I couldn't help but notice that your tipple has slipped from your fingers and come to grief. I am saddened for your loss, and do not judge you. I'm attuned to your emotions, and sense that you may be embarrassed. I'm here to help, perhaps I could arrange for your safe egress from this establishment? It's no trouble at all, I'd be only too happy to be of assistance. '

In the same instant that the sound of splintering glass rings through the air, the Pavlovian bogan lets its spirit flow.

'AAAAAAHAHAHAHAHAHA TAXI! SOMEONE GET THIS DICKHEAD A TAXI! TAXI! TAXI!'

Anti-intellectualism

The bogan will tell you it likes to think. However, prone to the unquestioning acceptance of prescribed religion and nationalism, its mental faculties are accordingly stunted. Anti-intellectualism is the bludgeoning device the bogan deploys against the nerds of the adult world. It affords the bogan the opportunity to validate its poorly-informed opinion on complex issues by stating that a lifetime of studying the subject at hand actually serves as an impediment to any ivory tower elitist's analysis. The bogan believes its knowledge of the 'Real World' (which is limited to *Today Tonight*, explosive domestic arguments, and last summer's trip to Dreamworld) trumps the intellectual's access to the university's considerable research resources and decades of wide reading within the field. This is because the bogan is a moron, but can't stand to be wrong, even about things it only has a passing interest in.

It all started in primary school when the young bogan realised that there were other kids much smarter than itself. This proved rather confusing for it. It could run faster, kick harder and jump higher than many of its counterparts, but why, then, could it not successfully multiply fractions or point out Japan on a map? Furious at its own inadequacies, and lacking the self-awareness or discipline to improve itself, the bogan lashed out the only way it knows how. Violently. It would hurl abuse such as 'smartarse', 'nerd' or 'teacher's pet', alluding to its classmates' superior intellectual traits, and, in the process, convince itself that they are intensely undesirable qualities. After all, nobody else in the class had jumped their dad's jet ski over the top of an unsuspecting swimmer. And it was only nine.

Flash forward some fifteen years. The bogue is gainfully employed in a job that requires it to wear a shirt and tie. The pay is reasonable, the receptionist has a super rack, and it is paying off a McMansion with multiple flat-screen televisions. Much to its chagrin, however, it turns out that its manager is like one of those nerds from back in school – someone chosen for their intellectual prowess, and who is therefore a smartarse. This manager not only earns twice as much as the bogan, but is also seeing the receptionist's super rack in the sack each night. Again, the bogan becomes very angry. Hatred coursing through its veins, it now decides that it loathes everything that has made the ugly nerd rich and successful. What follows is a lifetime of abject hostility and derision towards education, philosophy, literature, art, science, and anything else that it doesn't choose to understand. The bogan defiantly disregards these things as impractical and pointless, as its practitioners are a bunch of poofs who are oblivious to the bogan's xtremely real world.

Scapegoats

The bogan doesn't care if people it doesn't know die, unless they speak English and die in maxtreme quantities. Or they don't speak English but die in quantities so maxtreme as to depopulate a region of the planet. The time it will care most, though, is when deaths happen 'close to home', which is why the 2009 bushfires in Victoria and the insulation fires of 2010 have led to the bogan being deeply concerned for its own safety. And, oh yeah, other people's too.

In the trashmedia Kraken's frantic flailing for megajustice, someone to blame is found ASAP. Customarily, it's someone who has been blamed before. Politicians are popular, immigrants are ascendant and, of course, 'society' is never far from the limelight. Thankfully, the bogan is capable of holding others to higher standards than it expects from itself. The bogan will always love escapegoat.

Peter Garrett is a case in point. In his past incarnation as the frontman of Midnight Oil, Garrett was the happy recipient of a free pass from most bogans. Even though his politically charged lyrics may have borne a distinct whiff of political correctness gone mad, Garrett had to wait until they voted him in before he was derided for it. And even though many bogans vociferously deny the existence of something so patently ridiculous as the 'environment', Garrett was criticised as a sell-out and a hypocrite for making the leap from activist to pragmatist.

But it wasn't until early 2010, when Garrett inadvertently signed on as Minister Directly Responsible for Workplace Deaths, that he really copped it from the bogan. Despite the fact that insulation was installed in the homes of bogans who capitalised on the offer of cheap insulation without actually checking to see if the installer knew a pink batt from a pink bit, every death was Garrett's fault. The bogan's opinion about this was informed, then reinforced, by daily updates from Tracy Grimshaw, who, without so much as batting her reptilian eyelids, followed up with a story about dodgy tradies.

More recently, Christine Nixon, former Victoria Police commissioner, has experienced the bogan's righteous punishment. After realising that The Butterfly Effect was a pretty sick band *and* an Ashton Kutcher movie, it looked it up. As it turns out, when Christine Nixon sank her choppers into her chicken parmigiana at the pub one Saturday in February 2009, the displacement of parma air triggered a roaring gale 60 kilometres north-west of the pub, which fanned the flames to the extent that Sam the Koala needed to hit the bottle. The bogan knew that she must pay, and pay so much more than the $18 for the parma. The bogan wants her to never receive payment for anything ever again. It is likely to prevail.

Homophobia

The bogan will tell you it is open and tolerant. To scratch the surface of this claim, however, is to uncover pure, 24-carat bullshit. When challenged in an argument, the bogan will search its vocabulary for a stinging riposte, fail, and settle for a synonym of 'homosexual'. In bogan circles, this is as good as gold. The safety-conscious should note that synonyms for homosexual have been used before every known case of glassing in Australia. The bogan will use similar terminology when in a state of confusion or awkwardness about something it sees as a threat, or doesn't fully understand – whether that's someone being smart, expressive, refined, or in any way diverging from suburban boganic orthodoxy. If the bogan doesn't like something, it's for pooftas, because the bogan doesn't like pooftas or things that pooftas like. So during the bad times, when the bogan needs help in an argument, or merely comfort in unfamiliar circumstances, homophobia is there. The bogan male likes homophobia.

While bogan females may give more of an impression of being

tolerant of different sexualities, do not be fooled. Their enthusiastic pelvis-grinding and occasional attention-hungry pashing with other women on dance floors is primarily an attempt to increase their appeal to heterosexual bogan males. Any approaches by genuine lesbians will be met with the same horror a bogan male would regard a gay male's advance.

There are some notable exceptions to the bogan's homophobia – gays who have been provided defacto non-homo status, generally for services rendered to boganity. This includes former rugby league star Ian Roberts, and ex-Idol Anthony Callea (although the bogan will quickly point out that the latter's second record was 'totally gay'). Often the bogan will signpost its tolerance and openness to different sexualities by being able to identify various gay celebrities, and potential others that it claims are yet to 'come out of the closet'. The trashmedia Kraken has trained the bogan in how to engage in this type of speculation.

But despite how it might try to hide it when inconvenient, the bogan's homophobia is clear enough. If a straight male bogan is told that his hairdo is a bit gay, you can be sure that it will spend numerous minutes in the bathroom at the next opportunity, trying to carefully tousle the homosexuality out of his hair in the mirror, and fretting about whether his outfit is contributing to the problem. The bogan wishes to make itself as conspicuously un-gay as possible in life's various sexuality challenges, including approaching the urinal in the most manly way possible, and staring at the best available blank space of wall while standing around naked during a footy trip gang-bang.

Schadenfreude

When the bogan first heard of schadenfreude, it was very happy.
It thought it would finally have something to mix with Mother, Red
Bull having already been allocated exclusively to Jägermeister.
The bogan clapped excitedly; 'A MILF bomb!' it screeched. Its
excitement was shortlived, as schadenfreude is actually only a
concept, and the only concepts that truly intoxicate a bogan are
political correctness gone mad, free speech and confusion.

Despite this initial setback, it turns out that the bogan still likes
schadenfreude very much. While it will glass anyone that takes
pleasure at any of its own gaffes, the bogan will use its phone to
record anyone else's public humiliation, and then broadcast it to
Facebook as soon as possible.

While the bogan itself believes that it can never be blamed,
it derives maxtreme enjoyment from viewing the misfortunes of
other bogans. Other anyone, really. In particular, the bogan will
embrace the failings of celebrities most passionately of all. The
bogan has a curiously pathetic and symbiotic relationship with
celebrities, parasitically feeding off their success to validate their
stunted belief that one day people will give a shit what they do, yet,
like any parasite, leaping off its host the moment things get hairy.
Thus, Tiger Woods is now a tip rat, Paris Hilton a slut and Lindsay
Lohan a junkie. However, the bogan, deep down, knows that this
schadenfreude will not last, that it will forgive the celebrity and
reattach its life-giving appendages to its trashmedia intravenous
drip. Because it believes that it, too, is destined to face the rise
to fame, fall into sex addiction, and rise to bogan forgiveness one
day, hence his moments of schadenfreude are brief.

That goes for people the bogan knows, like Tiger Woods. When it comes to anonymous Australians, however, the bogan's capacity for mirth at the pain of another is limitless. While *Australia's Funniest Home Videos* show has been on Australian TV screens for two decades, the bogan is yet to grow tired of unruly farm animals biting fat women, children headbutting each other on malfunctioning playground equipment, and over-confident dads coming to grief on quad bikes – all to the same four 'boing' noises. The patriotic bogan deems viewing this procession of canned laughs as 'being able to laugh at myself', and the show's theme song ('Australia, Australia, this is you') agrees.

PUBLIC
SERVICE

Freedom of speech

Despite its understanding of patriotism being limited to Southern Cross tattoos, hating whoever the prime minister is, and the unwitting embrace of foreign cultural norms, the bogan cherishes each and every thing that it has seen in Australia's proposed Bill of Rights. No item is more important to the bogan than its right to freedom of speech. The bogan pauses to consider this, and then loudly pronounces something additional about its rights, and how freedom of speech is also in the Constitution. The bogan is a poor student of political history, as it is too busy being xtreme in the present. Xtremely free in its speech.

The boganic interpretation of this alleged freedom of speech allows the bogan to both internally and verbally condone the way that it is. It is proud to be uninformed, impulsive and vulgar, and it can't wait to exercise its divine entitlement to tell everyone all about it. As such an eclectic creature, this freedom takes many forms. Examples include loudly berating retail staff, undertaking heated domestic arguments in public, initiating 80 decibel phone conversations on public transport, participating in gutter journalism opinion polls, and proactively offering xenophobic or poorly considered opinions on society to whomever makes fleeting eye contact with the bogan. Triggering the bogan's freedom of speech button with this glance produces a feeling of regret similar to that experienced when accidentally using the word 'walk' within earshot of an attentive and easily excitable dog.

While certain that it should be a beneficiary of free speech, the bogan is equally adamant that it should not be a recipient of it. The bogan reacts poorly to a non-bogan passing judgement on it, angrily discrediting the opinion offered to it as political correctness gone mad, or some sort of cultural elitism that must be crushed. This also extends to criticism of its discombobulated tXt-speak, because literacy is a detestable condition confined to the enemies of the bogan. Evidently, this powerful freedom of speech wielded by the bogan has not sufficiently motivated it to learn to speak well. It reserves the right to speak in misnomers, flawed syllogisms and malapropisms, and not have anyone point this out to it.

Eventually, it becomes clear that to the bogan, freedom of speech is primarily confined to its own right to yell over the top of someone else, until it becomes agitated enough to glass them for being a c***.

Conspiracy theories/urban legends

The bogan knows things. It doesn't know how it knows; it just knows. Often, it's things that the general population is not aware of. Even more often, the bogan knows things when the information is presented to it in a Facebook group, a trusted news source, or in Andrew Bolt's column. The bogan just knows. The bogan's desire to lap up conveniently edited pieces of information and then parrot them back as the comprehensive truth is a conceptual comb-over capable of cladding even the baldest of theories in half-a-dozen tenuous strands of delusion. The bogan's ability to rapidly determine the true nature of things spares it from the need to learn the context, alternatives, or ramifications of any area of knowledge it turns its attention to. This renders the bogan more efficient than the rest of society, freeing up time for it to go out and be xtreme at awesome stuff while everyone else plods along like suckers.

Not content to just hastily weigh in on standard topics, the bogan seeks out preposterous claims that nobody else has ever heard of. Who could have known, for example, that the unassuming rodent-canine hybrid known as the Chihuahua can cure asthma, or that sneezing seven times in a row releases the same endorphins as when having an orgasm. The bogan knows these things.

Its insatiable need to know things also extends to more complex issues such as assassinations, the chemical composition of drinking water or the veracity of global warming. While the world's thinking community remains vexed, the bogan's verdict is in: climate change, for instance, is nothing but a 'Trojan Horse' for power-hungry scientists to force their big taxing, redistributive socialist green left agenda on 'hardworking Australians'. The bogan also seems convinced that much of the country's drinking water is contaminated 'with that filthy fluoride stuff', an assertion it will loudly bellow while cooking in its non-stick pan, hosing its Buddhist-iconography garden ornaments or cleaning its swimming pool (all being made from inorganic fluoride). The knowledgeable bogan will then espouse the safety benefits of drinking vitamin water while punching out an SMS at 110 kilometres per hour.

Further still, if a bogan sees evidence of a celebrity with a conspiracy theory, its truth value becomes gospel multiplied by max. The primary exception to this is the bogan's scepticism towards Tom Cruise and the Church of Scientology, which attract great boganic mirth. After all, Tom Cruise's aliens look different to the drawing that Uncle Mick did of the time that he saw martians after being offered a funny cigarette at the pub. In fact, Scientology is a sinister scheme devised by the government to channel taxpayer dollars into getting aliens to overthrow Palestine and steal all of the oil and feed Elvis to George Bush who is actually the guy from the *Da Vinci Code*. The bogan just knows.

Other people's backyards

The bogan staunchly defends its right to access middle-class welfare schemes such as negative gearing in order to create a highly geared and lowly diversified investment empire. Apartments, units, houses with big backyards – investment properties equal big, odiferous bogan schmackos. But while the bogan wants to own all properties, it also insists that other people retain them too. It wants other people to have backyards to adequately house things the bogan finds unpleasant.

While the bogan will reluctantly acknowledge the need for undesirable things like sewage farms, landfills, and non-franchised coffee shops to exist somewhere, it wants the consequences of its own rabid behaviour to be entirely borne by other people, far far away. The crucial problem here is that the bogan and its interests have colonised the majority of the nation. Very few locations exist where something such as a hospital could be built, due to an avalanche of bogan complaints that the sound of the ambulances would ruin the peace and quiet during their routine viewings of *Grey's Anatomy*. If an ailing bogan is not instantly cured by the medical system, the bogan's family will simultaneously phone *A Current Affair* and Slater & Gordon to extract maxtreme justice. The bogan wants to eat its cake, be given an unlimited free supply of additional cakes, and never get diabetes from the staggering volume of glucose contained therein. Or else.

The bogan considers proposed airports and nuclear dumps unacceptable, and medium density residential developments near its McMansion even worse. While the McMansion occupies 98% of its block of land, any development that proposes to do the same without a third rumpus room in its floorplan elicits intense existential fury in the bogan. The bogan fears that townhouses and apartments may attract latte-sipping intellectuals or ethnic minorities to its neighbourhood, placing the commercial viability of the local megachurch under threat.

Hordes of infuriated NIMBY bogans will descend upon the local municipal offices, declaring that this entire layer of government needs to be sacked immediately. They will drag the proposed development through an extended and costly planning appeals process, offering an array of excuses entirely ineffective at masking their own self-interest. Eighteen months, four lawyers, and six architectural redesigns later, the now utterly compromised development will proceed. The bogan will claim a *Castle*-esque victory over 'greedy developers', and gear up its negativity to resume complaining about how housing affordability is atrocious, making it unable to expand its negatively geared empire at the desired velocity.

Talking about joining the army

The bogan likes talking about things it never intends doing. Loudly.
The bogan's love of killing things is manifested in many ways; oversized pets, burning fossil fuels, paintball, and glassing c***s, but perhaps the most devoted bogan love is talking about joining the army. For there is nothing conceivably more maxtreme than talking about shooting an xtreme gun, in xtreme temperatures, in countries and terrain that it is xtremely unaware of. All in the name of the most xtreme of all causes: National Security. The very thought of talking about defending its shores and bestowing freedom on some funny brown-coloured people feeds its highly strung temperament like a tonic distilled from crack. The merciful

warrior, the apotheosis of freedom and soldier of peace, simply cannot wait to talk about joining the Armed Forces. Once its back recovers.

The bogan cannot actually join the army for a multitude of reasons. While the appeal of driving an enormous armoured vehicle is certainly undeniable, the bogan's normally unwavering enthusiasm for killing things seems strangely lacklustre when it comes to actually enlisting and becoming the thing. Upon deeper reflection, the reasons for such paucity of endeavour become even clearer. Neither Iraq nor Afghanistan boasts clubs where it can get loaded on Jagerbombs and glass c***s. But it fails to realise that both countries have abundant quantities of real bombs and its inhabitants can quite easily shoot c***s, should they so desire. There is also the issue of a distinct lack of flesh exposure among women in these war-torn lands. The bogan knows this and doesn't like it.

The bogan is never one to stray too far from its comfort zone, and the army requires it to do too many pesky things that get in its way. In a curious discord from its usual pit of ignorance, the bogan, it seems, realises that joining the army is nothing like being Jason Bourne. Or Matt Damon, for that matter. The bogan concludes this landmark glimmer of introspection by inwardly vowing to go and work in the mines, while continuing to verbalise a feigned plan to surpass Australia's victory at Gallipoli.

Shock jocks

The bogan clings to its habits like a mollusc to a shipwreck's hull. It will only holiday in places with familiar franchised retailers, it will only drink green beer on St Patrick's Day, and it will trust only

Richard Wilkins via satellite from Los Angeles. But sometimes the bogan grows tired of this predictability. It wonders if the highs and lows of life outside of its cocoon are worth experiencing. It craves xtreme emotion. At this point, the bogan will sometimes purchase a non-Jetstar international airfare, watch SBS News, or try something in wholemeal. Alarmed and confused by the ordeal, it concludes that it can have its desire for new horizons ably met in radio form by a myopic shock jock.

Kyle Sandilands not only discovered the fickleness of bogan rage when he ran the rape lie detector skit on Sydney radio, but also the graciousness of bogan forgiveness. The bipolar bogan was quick to pardon Sandilands, as its dwindling outrage was usurped by its growing need to be outraged again. Channel 7 soon restored Kyle to his rightful position of luring bogans onto talkback radio.

The Melbournian bogan, for years denied the true Sydney-style talkback radio experience, now has Talk Radio 1377. On AM, no less – the original bastion of bogan-baiting hate-mongers – this network features the crème de la crème of bogan-baiting hate-mongers. Here, among the company of Sammy Newman, Andrew Bolt and alcoholic ex-*A Current Affair* hatewright Chris Smith, the bogan can find rare refuge from the Political Correctness Gone Mad which is rampant throughout the latte-sipping media. The middle-aged and elderly bogans have been feeling as though they've been missing out, with the younger bogans enjoying their Ed Hardy clothes, *Australian Idol* and anal sex. There has for years been a simmering rage, lying dormant, and waiting to be activated by some old-fashioned mad hating skills.

Talk radio has the requisite skills to appeal directly to the bogan's hate gland. Where *A Current Affair* can only hint that Asians are invading the country, Andrew Bolt can say that multiculturalism 'rewards most those who integrate least'. Perhaps in good time, he will be able to fan the flames of a race riot, much as Alan Jones did in Cronulla. To the bogan, calling into talkback radio for a pause-poor skewed rant is the beginning, middle and end of 'doing something'. From there, it is perfectly positioned to blame everything on the government.

Paintball

Its mother cried that morning. The bogan son awkwardly embraced her, telling her that everything would be okay. He'd be back home safely soon enough, he said. And besides, he'd used a gun before, and could handle himself in a fight. His mother continued to weep, unconsoled. She had hoped never to see the day that her son would go off to paintball war. But she knew it was for a cause much greater than her own selfish need to see her only child be safe. It was for his best mate's buck's party.

Paintball's origins date back to the year that Phil Collins plagued the world with *In the Air Tonight,* and went on to sell a buttload of copies. There was definitely something in the air the night that shooting paint-filled capsules from a high-powered gun became a bogan rite of passage. To killing things. Embodying bogan-trusted loves of war and paint, paintball is a pseudo-deadly simulation of what will never happen on a real battlefield. Nevertheless, the bogan embraces it with the same fervour it musters up when talking about joining the army.

Pregnant with anticipation, the bogan eagerly awaits the impending skirmish with its ten best mates. What lies ahead is a day of shooting balls of paint at its mates' balls, with a particular emphasis on assassinating the buck. True to form, the bogan lacks the discipline to stay 'alive' or face any real consequences of being in a 'battlefield'. It will thus run around maniacally, gun in one hand and massive can in the other, scanning the terrain so it can repeatedly shoot the buck for the sixteenth time and prove once and for all that it is indeed the biggest and quickest guerrilla in the jungle. This, despite the fact that it was 'killed' about three minutes after strapping on its protective goggles. All the while, its mother sits alone in her lounge room, forlornly thumbing a tattered photo of her child while the clock ticks loudly from out in the hallway.

Some days later, when the paint has finally peeled off and the camouflage gear nicked, he will proudly display his extreme bruising to all and sundry. He will enthral his listeners with tales of gallantry and valour, and laugh uncontrollably about the time he totally 'nailed Dave in the balls, LOL'. Meanwhile, his life giver is relieved that her progeny is back safe and sound without getting killed or acquiring trench foot.

SARTORIAL SPLENDOUR

Tramp stamps

It's not news that a typical bogan is impulsive, vulgar, and eager to acquire gravitas and respect through superficial means, but it's an important part of why it has such a strong affiliation with artless tattooing. While there can sometimes be a blurred delineation between male and female bogan behaviour, nevertheless there remains some sort of desire for the female bogan to present herself with feminine elements. This is often manifested in the alarmingly liberal application of cheap cosmetics and female fragrances, along with apparel that betrays abundant information about her physique. After initial confusion as to how the female bogan could acquire tattoos while still retaining some semblance of femininity, the solution was found: tramp stamps.

The tramp stamp is a tattoo on the small of the female's back, typically between 4 cm × 4 cm and 10 cm × 10 cm, though some tribal specimens have been observed that cover the entire rear span of the muffin top. The female bogan seeks not warrior symbols such as skulls, flames or sporting team logos, making the list of acceptable designs quite short. It includes dolphins, butterflies and love hearts – images that deceptively suggest that the female would make a good mother. Another favourite is Asian lettering. In a notable departure from her usual discrimination against Asian people, she embraces their alphabets to convey lofty ideals such as hope, friendship and loyalty. Tribal patterns are also permitted, though they are typically less angular and robust than those found on the male.

Why the lower back? Possibly as a display of plumage while getting ploughed from behind, but more likely as a misguided attempt to be discreet. When the female bogan observes herself in the mirror, she typically only sees the front of her body. Lacking the self-awareness to realise that anyone standing behind her is observing the other side, she forms the opinion that she has found the ideal way to augment her appearance without sacrificing her perceived likeness to classier women. Also problematic is the female bogan's tendency to wear ill-fitting clothing, exposing large amounts of back real estate every time she bends over to belt her recalcitrant children.

Christian Audigier

Some suspect Christian Audigier is an arsehole. Yet the bogan loves him. Despite not knowing who he is. Despite being his personal billboard for years.

Mr Audigier is the plastic-faced French fashion designer who has unleashed the visual misery of not just Von Dutch but also Ed Hardy on cities worldwide. His technique is devastatingly simple: repackage Californian redneck pop art from the 1960s by printing it on hats and t-shirts, get some trashbag celebrities to wear it and then affix astonishingly high prices to the products. The bogan is willing to structure its entire month's wage around the acquisition of one of these products.

'Von Dutch' was actually a Californian mechanic and car pinstriper named Kenneth Howard, who worked from the 1950s until dying of alcoholism-related causes in 1992. His estate sold the rights to use his creative works to a Japanese conglomerate who then onsold them before they eventually wound up in the filthy paws of Audigier. The brand's time as genuine fashion was fleeting, before the bogan became aware of the brand and began paying $110 for a trucker cap or gaudy handbag bearing the logo.

Once the Von Dutch trend waned, Audigier returned with something even more obnoxious – Ed Hardy. Hardy is a Californian tattooist and artist who sold the rights to use his 1960s tattoo work in 2002, once again snapped up by Audigier, in 2004. The subsequent garments are emblazoned with retro tattooing (skulls, flames, predatory animals and other maxtreme motifs), bright metallic paint and glitter. T-shirts sell for between $150 and $250.

The bogan, like a moth to a light globe, is drawn to the opportunity to display fashionable torso tattooing at venues that demand the wearing of clothes. If the bogan is able to afford multiple Ed Hardy garments, it can also indulge its short attention span by donning a different garment the next day, and hence a new set of tattoos. Being able to display large tattoo art in a nightclub or shopping centre environment increases the confidence of the bogan, and makes it feel closer to Hollywood.

At the conclusion of the Ed Hardy fad, Audigier will retreat to his lair, flip through a retro pop art book and plan his next cynical attack on the hip pocket of the unwitting aspirational bogan.

Tribal tattoos

Much the same as a herd of warring goats, bogans closely associate success and social prominence with pursuits relating to physical prowess. Finding a convenient way to channel the spirit of the gladiator in order to become the alpha of their town or suburb can be critical to the self-worth of the bogan. The bogan has a vague awareness that over the millennia, there have probably been thousands of brave feats of killing things performed by warrior-like people. But, opening a book to figure out what, where, and when can be quite threatening. Thousands of bogans have discovered that a quick and effective way to appropriate the battle markings of this imagined warrior is through a tribal tattoo.

Tribal tattoos serve another important function for the bogan: they actually allow it to convince itself that it is culturally and artistically aware. Because tribes are probably from some other culture, the bogan becomes proud of its open-mindedness and ability to embrace the thuggish tendencies of an abstract people from another era and/or community. By doing so, the bogan displays tolerance and acceptance of all people, and deeply connects with the cosmos.

Secondly, tribal tattooing allows the bogan to express its artistic sensibilities. The bogan enjoys being able, upon enquiry about its tattoo, to state that he/she 'designed it myself'. Designing a tribal tattoo requires the capacity to draw up to 60 arced or swirled lines with no defined spatial or thematic structure, and to then pass it off as inspired expression. Just as this was within the capacity of the glistening trail of a snail on a slab of hot concrete, the bogan is also able to triumph in this endeavour. Jagged lines in the design depict battle-readiness, hardness, and other unspecified warrior traits.

The bogan male is aware that a tribal tattoo is best displayed on a broad, warrior-like piece of flesh. Some bogans will achieve this through making their biceps huge at the gym, while others will eat more fatty food than they ever should. The female bogan also expresses interest in acquiring tribal markings, though generally in the form of a tramp stamp.

By expressing itself through the permanent application of a tangle of unintelligible and meaningless lines to its body, the bogan attains the status of artist, creator, warrior and, perhaps most importantly, suitable breeding partner.

Southern Cross tattoos

As previously discussed, tattoos regularly adorn the bogan's body, advertising such things as warlike toughness, confected spirituality, femininity and cultural sensitivity. In the tradition of co-opting symbols it doesn't fully understand, the bogan *tatt du jour* is the Southern Cross. A beautiful and evocative design derived from the celestial formation of the same name, the Southern Cross appears on the Australian flag, and also on the flags of New Zealand, Brazil, Papua New Guinea and Samoa.

The bogan, considering itself patriotic, is actually a nationalist, and being unaware of the distinction between these two things, believes Australia has a monopoly over a constellation that is visible from about fifty other countries the bogan has never heard of. Subsequently, the Southern Cross tattoo, or the 'Aussie Swazie' as it's known in some circles, has become for the bogan a symbol of 'Aussie Pride', a secret bogan codeword for immense racial intolerance.

The Southern Cross tattoo comes in a number of forms, from the popular and simple five star design to those incorporating the outline of the Australian continent or a boxing kangaroo, and is sometimes adorned with such 'patriotic' slogans as 'Fuck off, we're full', 'We grew here, you flew here', and 'If you don't love it, leave'.

These slogans first came to the attention of the wider public during the 2005 Cronulla riots, started when local bogans became incensed that groups of Lebanese people were behaving like bogans on 'their' beach. The Aussie bogans attempted to send the Lebanese packing, but failed to make Cronulla even 1/100th as scary for Lebanese people as Beirut. Southern Cross tattoos have been proliferating in Australia ever since. TBL's tattooist sources claim to be churning out about 15 Aussie Swazies a week, a startling pace which shows no sign of slowing.

So, as the sun sets on another day of being a proud Aussie, the bogan looks towards the skies only to be baffled by the strange appearance of a constellation that looks like a possum sitting in a tree. It quickly ignores this astronomical anomaly, briefly glances at its tattoo and continues to scan the landscape for any stray Lebanese.

Fashion statements

The term 'fashion statement' is an interesting one. It suggests that a person's choice of clothing says something about themselves, what they think, and how they see the world. Basically it's a speech bubble connected to one's body all day long, visible to everybody. So it makes perfect sense that people should wear clothing that they understand. The bogan does not make perfect sense.

Bogans are particularly fond of wearing clothes with large numbers printed on them. One possible explanation is that it's an intellectual statement about what the bogan feels to be an excessively competitive culture in which everyone is made to feel as though they are in a race. This possibility can safely be eliminated, as the bogan does not think in those kinds of abstract symbolism. After careful thought, TBL can conclude that no explanation can possibly justify this behaviour. It is therefore just baseless trend-trotting and a desire to wear something written in large, bright lettering.

The confusion does not end there, though. The bogan also enjoys wearing clothing that randomly pairs a foreign city name with a random noun and a random number. If you ask a dilettante bogan why it is wearing a yellow t-shirt with 'San Francisco Bears 74' scrawled across it, do not expect to get an answer that contains actual insight. If you press further and ask it what its favourite spot in San Francisco is, the poorly travelled bogan will likely become agitated. And any suggestion that San Francisco is America's leading gay town, and that 'bear' is slang for 'overweight and hairy gay man' is certain to create a punch-on.

This trend of boganic fashion non-statements is happening on streets and dance floors near you. Even in Melbourne's non-bogan friendly 'hipster precinct', a TBL haunt, a bogan male was recently sighted wearing a 'Fretilin' emblazoned fitted t-shirt made by mid-price disposable 16–25 fashion brand M-One-11. In the course of TBL's research, the bogan was asked whether he thought Xanana Gusmão had been an effective president for the Timorese. It took a good 30 seconds to explain to the irritable bogan that he was wearing a politicised t-shirt relating to a country that he could not have pinpointed on a map, OMG, and knew nothing about. The bogan's fashion statement can be summarised as 'duh'. Just look at Ed Hardy.

Movember

Movember has for some years been an initiative to raise money for, and awareness of, men's health issues via the growing of moustaches in the month of November. Several years after the event's conception, upon seeing celebrities participating, the bogan male caught wind. Its belated arrival did nothing to hamper its enthusiasm. In fact, the excitement was such that the bogan had little time to stop and learn the rationale behind the moustache-growing phenomenon. And there was no need to. Andrew G was doing it. Everyone was doing it. Therefore the bogan would do it too.

Now comfortable enough to go bush with the protection of the herd, the bogan set about growing a moustache in November for no reason other than the irresistible portmanteau created by substituting the letter 'M' for 'N'. People would be impressed, the bogan reasoned, at the wit and spontaneity required to be involved in a movement with such a clever name.

Having a moustache made the bogan feel like a seventies porn star, and this made it okay for the bogan to act like a seventies porn star: a green light for a month of seedy behaviour, innuendo and jokes about cleaning the pool. It also gave the bogan a chance to advertise that it had indeed gone through puberty, showing off its manly plumage in an effort to impress the bogan female. Invariably, the bogan will select the handlebar moustache as its style of choice, consistent with its life philosophy that more is always more. Like a herd of competing caribou, social pecking orders for the month are determined by the size and ferocity of the handlebar face-antler on the bogan.

During the course of the month, the bogan saw other Movember participants actively fundraising for men's health, and consequently receiving the approval of others. This convinced it to announce that it was doing the same. Any actual offers of money were met with confusion, with the bogan tending to pocket any proceeds for its own use.

At Movember's end, the bogan is confused. By now comfortable with its well-developed moustache and accompanying one-liners, it decides to continue with its new look. Moustache numbers around it drop sharply in the days that follow, and young bogan women return to their default position of decrying the lip warmer in accordance with the prevailing Hollywood fashion. That evening the bogan male shaves, and rejoins its herd.

Suiting up

On the surface, much of the male bogan's behaviour portrays a deep resentment of 'intellectuals', 'elitists', and successful people who are not celebrities or lottery winners. But this is merely a manifestation of what is arguably its greatest fear: being left out. Indeed, the bogan male aspires to a high society life of sophistication, being in the know about get-rich-quick schemes and dalliances with corporate lawyer-cum-lingerie models. But, lacking the required self-discipline and rigour to achieve genuine success, it resorts to trying to convince itself that it is a part of elite society by 'suiting up' once in a while for a major event such as the Melbourne Cup, a wedding or its little sister's deb. This also allows the bogan the opportunity to do two things it likes very much: pretend it is a celebrity at a red carpet event; and use the phrase 'suit up'.

Men's formal wear is traditionally worn in a conservative, understated fashion, seeking to subtly connote traits such as respect, confidence and power. But that stuff is for poofs. The bogan is not conservative or understated, and seeks to convey an image of maxtreme human billboard branding at all times. As Armani is yet to produce a suit conspicuously splashed with logos and bogan slogans, the bogan male has had to find other ways to signpost its alpha-consumer bogan herd member status when suiting up. Its 'anything you can do I can do . . . bigger' attitude has led it to remix its formal attire into an eye-jarringly garish combination of garments consisting of: black suit, black shirt, white 'crocodile skin' shoes, shiny silver tie, topped off by an enormous pair of European designer sunglasses. The end result is an awkwardly clad creature that looks somewhere between a confused penguin and an ill-assembled piano.

At the conclusion of a night's formal festivities, the piano-penguin bogan male has lured a shiny orange female bogan, shoes in hand, back to its lair. He is horrified when she asks him to suit up.

SEX

Sexpo

Once a year, all of the bogan's tawdry sexual fantasies come to bear under one large corrugated roof. Deviously marketed as an exhibition focusing on all aspects of health and sexuality, Sexpo is but a filthy menagerie of sweat, failed dreams, washed-up porn stars and overpriced dildos. Nursing love-toy sample bags and blank faces, the bogans patiently peruse everything, from stalls hawking the latest in pleasure-inducing gadgetry to Miss Nude Australia presiding over two men simulating sexual positions from the *Kama Sutra* on a blow-up doll. Languidly strolling past the gaudy bazaar of g-strings, giggles, porn mags, peepshows and motorised parachute rides, the bogan's mind is briefly distracted by the sudden appearance of a man dressed as a giant penis handing out lube and condoms.

Not to be left out of the action, the female bogan will enthusiastically participate in the 'Fake an Orgasm' competition or take pole dancing lessons or bare all in the Amateur Strip Show, all the while being cajoled by the aural charms of timeless bogan Russell Gilbert. This further gives the bogan an opportunity to attempt to temporarily apply the ADHD ethos of pornography to its own sex life. By interacting with B-grade porn stars and obtaining a signed copy of Monica Mayhem's *Anal Episodes 9: The Ploughing at Bathurst*, it satisfies its need to immerse itself in the seedy, illicit underground of hardcore erotica.

Of course, no bogan event is complete without the gratuitous burning of massive amounts of fossil fuels. Enter the group of daredevil freestyle motorcyclists who call themselves the Crusty Demons. Their ability to jump repeatedly over mounds of sand on a 250 cc dirt bike while performing strange tricks has the bogan gasping in amazement as it vicariously taps into the bone-chilling, high-octane excitement. Once it has collected a sufficient number of free samples, it will make one last round of the garish collection of adult products that can be found at any suburban Club X store before scurrying home to ferociously masturbate.

Hugh Hefner

In your more private moments, you probably enjoy looking at some porn. The animalistic, overplayed instant gratification world of adult entertainment can be a (re)productive escape. The bogan is not like you. It wants to experience this world at all times. The internet has made porn footage easily accessible, but the bogan females wanted something more 'tasteful' to communicate their raunchy life-vision at the shopping centre and the pub. As a result, they turned to the sexual fantasies of an 83-year-old American man. Please vomit in your mouths as we explain how this is a manifestation of . . . feminism. Of all things.

There have long been two opposing camps in the feminist movement, one arguing that pornography is degrading, and one arguing that it advances a woman's freedom of expression and sexuality. Without being aware of this, the bogan female has decisively sided with the movement that best allows it to be crass. Some commentators have attempted to apply the lofty metaphor of women 'repossessing the oppressive world of porn and making it their own', but this gives too much credit to the thought process of the female bogan.

We already know that the male bogan has a clumsy, manic sense of sexuality. It craves the maxtreme, indulging it through faux-lesbianism, the use of expensive and brightly coloured props, the viewing of hardcore porn, or pressuring its partner into taking it up the shitter. The same primal appeal lies in the expansive, glittering faux-tough branding of 'couture' clothing such as Ed Hardy. It has taken a rickety octogenarian to merge these two bogan loves, feeding smut and glitter into his finely tuned bogan and redneck merchandising machine, and miraculously churning out a feminist statement at the other end. The Playboy brand has transformed itself in the mind of the female bogan from 'crude' to 'cheeky', a delineation that the bogan has little grasp of.

Today, every second bogan female can be seen tottering around as walking billboards for Hefner's concept of sexy. Playboy has created a wide range of mid-priced, prominently branded products for all facets of the female bogan's life, and they have been purchased in abundance. A cover for her iPhone? Sure. A whale tail frame for her tramp stamp? Yep. In her more private moments, she closes her eyes and imagines seductively feeding a cluster of Viagra tablets to Hugh Hefner in the Playboy mansion, like a Roman peasant with a bunch of grapes for her emperor. A truly liberated feminist.

Anal

In your private moments with your significant other, casual nocturnal acquaintance, or even with a random from the pub, you may explore the fullness of your sexuality. It's a modern world, and taboos are dropping. 'Anything between consenting anybodies', as Marvin Gaye so eloquently put it.

But not for the bogan male. He believes it exists purely to bust taboos, if not hymens. He goes straight up the date.

Seasoned by years of cramp-inducing porn consumption,

the bogan male no longer has a concept of a healthy sexual relationship. It must now dominate sluts. It must place its engorged member in as many inappropriate holes as it can conceive of (three) while shouting 'Take it, bitch!' and slapping her on the backflaps. The bogan exists to put the xxx in maxxxtreme.

The women's movement of the sixties and seventies transformed the world's ideas of how to do the deed. Pleasuring women became equally important to pleasuring the man. If the standard – missionary – position fails to achieve an orgasm for the woman, it should no longer be standard. Creativity and sensitivity are required. Unfortunately, because of the debilitating effect of porn on the bogan male's reality, and its butter-smeared grasp on human intimacy, meaningful relationships and women generally, the bogan has a fierce desire only for maxtreme fucking. Xtreme max double-penetrative sex is the only sex. The bogan wishes to live out the narratives presented on its computer screen by Randy Cockburger.

The bogan will approach sexual encounters initially as an opportunity to live out the dream promised to it in *Ten Things I Ate About Poo*, whereby he merely nods his head, draws his pork sword (he did on the footy trip), and proceeds to slap a woman around the head with it. 'Here it is, get at it, ho', proclaims the bogan male, embodying a glorious hybrid of Ron Jeremy and Charlie Sheen. When this approach fails, he adopts the James Bond model, assuming that his suave exterior and debonair behaviour (quips derived from last week's edition of *Zoo Weekly*) will simply result in an acquiescent corporate lawyer-cum-lingerie model falling blindly into bed with him. 'Is that a mirror in your pocket? Because I can see myself in your pants'.

Finally, he falls back on the tried and true bogan combination of eight vodka cruisers, half an hour of intense begging, and the promise of three extra charms for her Pandora bracelet. The bogan female, meanwhile, has had the concept of xtreme anal normalised in her social group ever since Tiarnee said that her boyfriend promised her a Tiffany's bracelet after she let him have a go at her arse. This bracelet has never been sighted.

While the heterosexual bogan male loves to absolutely jackhammer the crap out of every 'forbidden' female hole he can find, it goes without saying the bogan's own anus is, to use engineering parlance, a bridge too far. This is because the bogan is terrified of the concept that there are some men who prefer to share their parlour of pleasure with other men. The bogan, whose repertoire of witty insults is made up entirely of tired synonyms for 'homosexual', considers homosexuality strange and unnatural, yet is perfectly happy to rub one out while watching videos of girls fisting each other.

In the moments directly after his maxx orgasm, the Jeremy/ Sheen bogan is perplexed – is she asleep, or has she merely fallen into a coma of intense ecstasy? Or has his gentle donkey punch completely rendered her unconscious?

Cross-dressing

Cross-dressing has a long and noble history dating back to the invention of clothes, and has sometimes been used for disguise, sometimes for theatre, sometimes for scaring the shit out of people, and sometimes simply because it just feels right. More recently, it has come to be associated with drag queens and gay culture at large, things that your garden variety bogan feels a profound anxiety around. Subsequently, until recently, it would have been unthinkable that the bogan, known for deriding anything it finds anathema as 'gay', would admit to liking cross-dressing. But this has all changed. Now, no *Footy Show* segment, boys' weekend or bogan buck's party is complete without a male bogan dressing up as a woman. So how do we explain this flummoxing conundrum? Simple. It's not about the dress; it's about the balls underneath.

The bogan male dresses up as a woman to make a statement, which goes something along the lines of 'Hey, I'm wearing a dress, but I'm still the dominant ape, and if you call me a poof you'll cop a glassing worse than Wayne Carey's ex-missus.' Unlike traditional cross-dressing, which aims to project upon a man the impression of womanhood, bogan cross-dressing aims to project upon the man yet more manhood. This is why it is important for the bogan male that when it dresses up as a woman, it must look nothing like a woman. The cross-dressed bogan will pick a gown no actual woman would ever wear, deepen its voice, sit with its legs wide apart, belching and scratching its reproductive equipment regularly, and stroking the cultivated stubble it has grown for a number of weeks in preparation for the coming androgyny gauntlet. Any makeup used is smeared across the face, resulting in a kind of impressionistic, demented clown mask, a selfconscious effort to prove to other bogans that the cross-dresser has absolutely no expertise in its application, and is therefore not gay.

Being a bogan herself, often the female bogan will actually think that the sight of Rusty's leg hair spraying grotesquely through his fishnets is an ingenious and creative subversion of his actual gender (male). While the female bogan is no virtuoso at makeup application herself, she takes solace from the fact that the male's cosmetics are marginally more gaudy, overwrought, and clumsily applied than her own. Feeling a confusing mix of sympathy and maternalism, the bogan female resolves to reward its comically androgynous partner with the chance to do her up the arse at the end of the night. The homoerotic symbolism of this idea proves to be far too much for the stiletto-clad male bogan, who was already operating dangerously close to its irony threshold. The suddenly furious male rips off its wig, barks at its missus, and storms back to its male friends to plot some poofter bashing. Never again, until next time.

Cougars

Thanks partly to government health and safety initiatives (collectively referred to by the bogan as 'the nanny state'), and despite its best efforts, the male bogan is taking longer to die than ever before. Even the most xtremely safety-averse bogan has to keep its jet ski away from swimming areas, has airbags in its Chevrolet Commodore, and will be denied service at bars when it looks like it is smashed enough to glass one of its brethren. But while the nanny state is aiding the bogan to survive for longer, it has so far failed to make meaningful progress in helping the male bogan mature mentally as it ages. As a result of this, the female bogan realised that in order to attract a bogan alpha male, she had to look and act like a 20-year-old throughout her lifespan. So, like an already haggard hatchling emerging belatedly from a discoloured egg, the cougar was born.

An American TV show called *Cougar Town* premiered on Channel 7 in February 2010, featuring a 45-year-old Courtney Cox with an 18-year-old son. Cox plays a divorcee who decides to pursue a series of younger men. This was a light globe moment for the bogan female, who had previously suspected that Demi Moore's accomplishment was impossible for them to imitate. The bogan cougar set out to offset Hollywood's financial advantages by levering itself into muffin-top-generating hipster jeans, and head butting its makeup cupboard until taking on an unsettling shade of orange. Now ready to go on the prowl, the cougar begins shamelessly hunting through local nightspots for any remaining shards of what it remembers to be its glorious youth, in the process discarding what remains of its dignity.

After being informed of the term cougar, the bogan male's next few hours are entirely occupied by laughing at how cougar is also the name of one of its favourite mixed drinks, and a maxtreme toothsome cat. After a few of said drinks, the enterprising bogan male's mind turns to how he might be able to bed a cougar. The beastly female, not the beastly feline. Bogan males aged between 16 and 26 have concluded that it's totally hardcore to hook up with vastly older women, claiming 'they know what they want', and under the assumption that they all look like Courtney Cox. They do not.

Thus, when faced with a cougar in the flesh, the male suddenly reconsiders its initial enthusiasm. As the cumbersome quatrogenarian lumbers across the bar to pounce, the bogan begins to fret, casting its eyes left and right, looking for escape, but its packmates are on either side, egging it on, reminding it that it was 'in'. The next morning it wakes up next to a pillow stained a queer shade of orange with dark blue patches, slides out of bed and out the door. And never speaks of cougars again.

Sex addiction

The bogan likes having someone else to blame. This is the default strategy for mitigating its inability to manage its own behaviour. Celebrities also worked out some time ago that they can be excused from blame in this manner. So in an attempt to more effectively adopt the morally bankrupt ethos of *Two and a Half Men*, the bogan seeks to bed as many massive canned blondes as possible. A maxtreme sex life is the only sex life a bogan could want. And like Charlie Sheen himself, the bogan is pleased to be able to blame this sexual compulsion on a credible-sounding quasi-medical phenomenon – sex addiction. While the bogan may not be sufficiently equipped to ponder the troubled epidemiology of addiction, the bogan knows that sex addiction offers a convenient justification for its seedy promiscuity. After all, the next (il)logical step from its love for spurious allergies is the love for spurious and clinically dubious compulsions. Sex addiction is definitely the bogan's favourite fake addiction. After all, it is the faux addiction du jour in the celebrity world.

While the bogan may feign outrage at the prospect of an immensely beddable, world-famous, thirty-something billionaire celebrity cheating on their partner, it will proceed to forgive them and realise that it also suffers from the same crippling condition. So when it finds itself repeatedly self-administering the Stranger one Friday night, it does so safe in the knowledge that it shares the same ailment that allowed Tiger Woods to cheat on his wife. The endless and mysterious quest for 'tapping that' is finally a medical condition, much like leprosy or gout. And the bogan is well and truly afflicted.

Successful marketers are quick to milk the potential of a bogan/celebrity crossover, and have previously seen good returns from selling elaborate 'cures' for the bogan's fictional conditions. Upon learning that David Duchovny's raging sex drive was quelled by a self-help book, the bogan will happily drop $49.99 for a copy of *Out of the Shadows: Understanding Sexual Addiction*, and wishes it too could sign up for a $60,000, six-week treatment program somewhere in California, simultaneously being titillated by tales of infidelity featuring Hollywood's hottest and horniest. Alas, this is but a dream, and the bogan is destined to continue suffering under its crippling sex addiction. It must go on sharing its parlour of boganic pleasure with as wide a range of sexual desperados as it can lure home from suitable glassing barns.

SOCIAL MILIEU

Underbelly

It had crime, it had violence, it had drug use, it was based on some semblance of fact, it was on commercial television, and it was absolutely loaded to the brim with heavily stylised, semi-explicit sex scenes and exposed breasts. It was, in short, the televisual equivalent of bogan heaven.

Underbelly, for the uninitiated, was Channel 9's attempt to dramatise the story of Melbourne's 'crime war' during the 1990s and 2000s. With breasts. During this war, several heretofore unknown criminals became household names. To the bogan, 'household name' is entirely synonymous with 'celebrity'. And the only thing bogans love more than celebrities is celebrities playing celebrities.

Even better, *Underbelly* was packaged by its creators as highbrow entertainment, and the banning of the program in Victoria lent it the perfect level of illegitimate cred. And it had loads of breasts. Professionally and slickly filmed, it was frenetic enough to withstand the bogan's extraordinarily short concentration span, while simultaneously giving the impression of intellectual legitimacy. It thus became the bogan equivalent of the ABC's *Janus*, *Blue Murder* or *Phoenix*. Bogans are unaware of those shows.

It was so successful, in fact, that Channel 9 began immediately hunting down other criminals in order to expose Australia's bogans to a second series of actors holding guns and fondling/leering at breasts. Thus, *Underbelly 2: A Tale of Two Cities* pushed further back into the seventies, when the story was less interesting, the criminals less famous, and Australians had to watch Matthew Newton. And a pair of delightful New Zealand breasts. Then, there was season three: *The Golden Mile*, in which Channel 9, having run out of legitimate serious criminals to focus on, added breasts to a rehash of *Blue Murder* from 1995.

Then, in May 2010, Channel 9 announced plans to produce the fourth series of *Underbelly* IN 3D! This season is already being filmed, while season five has also been confirmed. Channel 9 has also green-lighted three telemovies based on similar events. The bogan cannot get enough of criminals. Or breasts.

This has, in turn, exposed a nascent urge in the nouveau bogan: the irrepressible desire to associate themselves with said underworld figures. The bogan will, upon an *Underbelly*-related conversation beginning, immediately and enthusiastically offer an anecdote about how, when they were employed at a café, they worked with a guy who once served a coffee to the table that Mick Gatto was sitting at. And that he seems like 'a top guy'.

Breasts.

The Corbys

In 2004, Schapelle Corby was a blue-eyed, moderately attractive Gold Coast TAFE student. A 20-something girl with a remixed name, dodgy family and a tendency to go to Bali for holidays. An exemplary new bogan. Things went badly wrong for her when she was convicted by Indonesian authorities of smuggling 4.2 kilograms of cannabis into Bali. Bogans back in Australia were outraged, and *Today Tonight/A Current Affair* realised that a major meal ticket had arrived. The other thing that arrived was a white Mercedes with an oversized front grill and a high-pitched screech emanating from its throat.

The bogan is a fiercely tribal creature, neatly tucking its selective disregard for truth into the pseudo-noble Australiana slogan of 'standing by your mates'. This egocentric 'us versus them' mentality permits the bogan to violate the laws of other jurisdictions whenever and however it wants, declaring foreign countries 'un-Australian' whenever problems occur.

At these times, the Australian government is supposed to spring into diplomatic overdrive to extricate the sullen bogan from the consequences of its wilfully ignorant alleged actions. An opportunistic celebrity lawyer will work pro bono to coach the bogan on crying, temporarily converting to Islam, or other methods with a chance of perverting the course of justice. The fortunate bogan eventually comes home to a hero's welcome and a lucrative 'tell all' *ACA* interview, having not learned a single thing (aside from the crying). All of this overrides the simple fact that in all likelihood the bogan in question travelled to a foreign country with draconian anti-drug laws while importing or taking illicit drugs.

The bogan regularly gains self-esteem from loudly declaring a stance on topics that it knows little about, and the idea of a healthy bogan female of reproductive age being imprisoned on a drug-related charge in an Islamic country represented the convergence of a number of its fears. It demanded that the Australian government 'do something' to bring Schapelle home.

The fact that her father and two of her half-brothers all had prior drug convictions was deemed by the bogan to be unrelated to Schapelle's certain innocence, along with piles of other incriminating evidence. It just knew. Meanwhile, Schapelle's sister Mercedes used her new fame to pop up and net $50,000 for stripping down for bogan bible *Ralph* magazine, airbrushed and spray tanned to within an inch of her life. This allowed the bogan readers to remark that 'I'd take that Mercedes for a spin', to the laughter of their similarly brain-dead mates.

While there are thousands of people imprisoned on drug-smuggling charges around the world, and hundreds of medical and social problems that cost the lives of Australians every year, the bogan sees no inconsistency in ignoring them all, save for Schapelle. It proudly participates in newspaper and television polls to 'confirm' Schapelle's innocence, vehemently maintaining to this day that a great injustice has been done.

Joining moronic Facebook groups

The bogan likes to belong. It also craves a sense of order and purpose.
The emergence of social networking spaces such as Facebook have given the bogan the means to indulge this higher order need to a spectacular degree. It can now proudly pledge its allegiance to a dizzying array of asinine interests, as long as it is worded in bad grammar and has at least two misplaced apostrophes.

Inexorably, the bogan will gravitate towards groups that have in excess of 10,000 members, a reassuring sign that the majority is on board its *Titanic* of dreams. The flotsam ranges anywhere from uninformed social/political causes (*Save Schapelle Corby/Don't let Sudanese refugees in/In Australia we eat meat, drink beer and speak FUCKIN ENGLISH*), to harebrained irony (*I have joined way too many groups since the layout has changed*), to stationery (*I love bubble wrap*) or to a simple expression of the will to live (*I do not want to be eaten by sharks/I love not being on fire*). There is also the non-political cause, such as *I will name my son <insert stupid comic book name> if this group reaches 10,000.*

Even more, the bogan will join groups that simply state

something utterly banal, but allows the bogan to feel better that they are not the only one who appreciates the cool touch of an unused pillow case on hot summer skin. Here is a brief list (please assume that the bulk of these are followed by [sic]):

- *I hate stupid people.*
- *Sitting in your towel after a shower because you're too lazy to get dressed.*
- *NO HAT, NO PLAY . . . ruined my lunchtime!*
- *Deliberately driving slower when being tailgated.*
- *Hot showers.*
- *Throwing paper balls in the bin.*
- *The sound and smell of rain.*
- *Scribbling the pen until it works.*
- *I use my cell phone to see in the dark.*
- *Going to the footy.*
- *I hate private number calls.*
- *I LOVE THE WEEKEND.*
- *Using the laptop in bed.*
- *I need a vacation!!!*
- *A warm, cosy bed.*
- *TEXTING!*
- *Sleeping with one leg out of the covers.*
- *I flip my pillow over to get to the cold side.*
- *Not being on fire.*
- *Looking in the fridge, then the cupboard, then the fridge, then giving up.*
- *I hate when I wake up and realise my dream wasn't real.*
- *Blasting music when you're home alone.*
- *Drunk texting.*

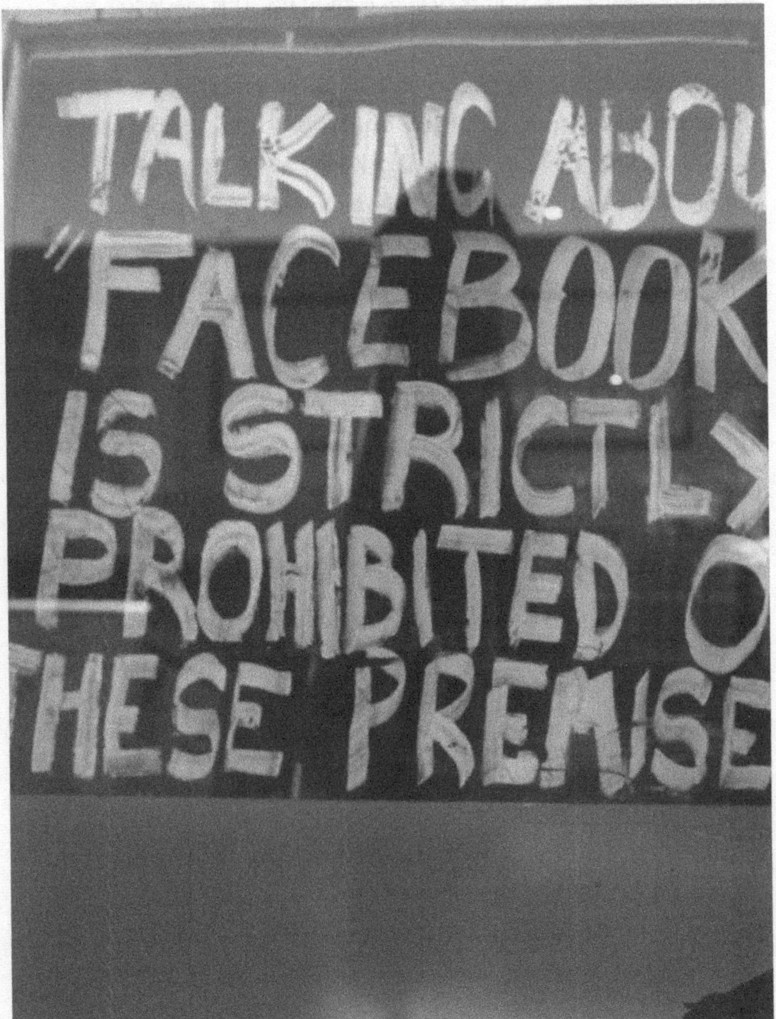
TALKING ABOU
"FACEBOOK
IS STRICTLY
PROHIBITED O
THESE PREMISE

The bogan will then use this space to post one comment, generally in fervent agreement with the page's thrust, then proceed to completely forget that they ever signed up. This leads to a new, surefire bogan-identification method, thanks to the good folk at Facebook and their new Orwellian 'privacy' settings. Simply click on the profile of a suspected bogan. Check for the number of groups the person is a member of, or pages they are a 'fan' of. There is, of course, a clear correlation between the number of pages listed, their inanity, and the individual's level of web-savvy boganinity.

Eventually, the bogan becomes a member of a critical mass of pointless groups that allow the discerning observer to accurately define the particular type of fuckwit they are dealing with. Thus, an individual that is a part of the *I responded to your text in two seconds, stop taking two hours to answer* group should be avoided just like that pesky backpacker hawking dolphin safety. Like a dirty fingerprint, the bogan swipes an attempt at uniqueness, only to signal to the world which types of ignorance and stupidity it cherishes the most.

Another option is joining the Facebook group for a blog about Things Bogans Like, proceeding to ignore the blog that the Facebook page was created to promote, then posting inane comments on the Facebook page that fundamentally revolve around the fact that bogans are, in their estimation, poor people.

However, its highly limited attention span will ensure the transience of the bogan's affiliations. One minute it joins *I like playing FarmVille*, and just as it ponders signing up to *Hot showers are awesome*, it has decided that it now belongs to *I don't like playing FarmVille* – all in the space of 15 minutes. It will then get bored with joining groups, and resume its game of FarmVille.

Glassing c***s

Bogans, in their search for dominance over others, will always seek out the weapon of maxtreme violence. However, the impulsive nature of the violence, when filtered through the constraints of their congenitally limited concentration span, dictates that the weapon must be sourced within arm's reach. Also, while many male bogans believe they have a close personal connection to Australia's (now celebrated) underworld, they lack access to anything beyond a kitchen knife. Thus, the shattered beer glass was elevated above the pool cue – the tool of the early bogan – to the nouveau bogan's weapon of choice.

And the bogan won't glass just anyone. In order to justify, in its strangely twisted moral compass, the commission of xtreme violence, the victim must be . . . a c***. This appeals to the bogan's reptilian desire to take things to the xtreme, physically, sartorially, linguistically. The bogan has run out of swearwords. This is odd, because the bogan, while a late adopter in almost all things, is nothing short of a market leader when it comes to expletives.

Once upon a time, the bogan could toss around 'dickheads' and 'wankers' with gay abandon, yet remain on the profane cusp of swearing trends. But today, despite being a member of several Facebook groups advocating proud nationalism and decrying the cultural creep of the US via TV, the bogan embraces whichever foul word is uttered by Carl Williams in *Underbelly*.

Lacking the creativity of other foul-mouthed subcultures to invent curses, they simply adopt whichever curse word finds itself on the tube. For example, as soon as Bruce Willis quoted old Westerns to some German motherfucker in *Die Hard*, the bogan had an entirely new weapon in its arsenal.

Soon enough, motherfucker was passé. Pretty much all swear words became banal, losing their threatening, offending impact. There was only one left. Thus, in short order, and prompted by its brief appearance in two films about criminals, the bogan had no choice but to start labelling everyone who it disliked/disagreed with 'c***' (or a fag/homo/poof). And then to glass the c***.

The only real option the bogan has today when spewing bile at its intended victim is to bludgeon them with sheer volume and weight of vitriol. 'What the fuck's your fucken problem, you fucken c***?' screams the enraged, inebriated bogan, simultaneously shattering his half-empty schooner and brandishing it unsteadily in the face of some guy who came perilously close to bumping into him on his way to empty his bladder. 'You got a fucken problem? You c***?'

Mobs

The bogan is never wrong about anything. In instances where there are negative consequences, a scapegoat must be found. The bogan will always seek to blame an outside factor, such as intellectuals, the government, the police, or ADHD. But what about the moral dilemma when the bogan wishes to initiate negative behaviour from scratch, and there's nothing else to blame?

Fortunately for the bogan, its lack of original thought means that there are usually other bogans who feel the same way as it does. So when it's time to cause trouble, the bogan will not hesitate to shoehorn the Australian cliché of 'standing by your mates' into the idea of 'let's form an angry bogan mob and cause maxtreme criminal damage'. Once the bogan integrates itself into an angry mob, its inhibitions melt away like polar ice caps. Liberated from its obligation to think, it duly charges around the place like a demented bronco, revelling in the collective unconsciousness. It is now free to steal any items that it may want, and destroy items that don't warrant stealing. The bogan at this point will feel a deep and personal sense of affiliation with the Eureka Flag, which it knows is associated with bogan ancestors 'not takin' shit from no one', but little detail beyond that.

A prime example of bogan mob behaviour occurred in suburban Melbourne in March 2010. After learning that the 'Easternats' burnout festival at Calder Park had been cancelled due to a commercial disagreement between organisers, the bogans decided that a franchised store of one of the sponsors (and over 30 kilometres from the Easternats site) was the logical place to protest. It was initially peaceful, but a critical mass of discontented bogans was soon assembled in one place. This resulted in windows being smashed in with steel poles, fully sick rims being looted from the store, and the store's ute getting overturned by a surprisingly collaborative bogan effort.

A newspaper photographer was at the scene, and some bogans took it upon themselves to kick the shit out of him for daring to photograph them. The photographer noted that police walked past without helping him up, as did a *Highway Patrol* reality TV camera crew who were deliriously excited to be filming a bogan mob of this size for future broadcast to other bogans.

While Ballarat's 1854 goldminers were protesting in mob form for the right to vote, the right to purchase land, and for taxation reform, the 2010 bogan was protesting in mob form for the right to have someone else pay to organise a place for it to do sick burnouts and hot laps to coincide with a Christian religious holiday. They truly are kith, if not kin.

Pre-mixed drinks

The bogan's love for shortcuts has been covered in reasonable sufficiency. What has not been talked about, however, is its curious love for overpriced saccharine poison, known as the alcopop. Notwithstanding the painfully unimaginative portmanteau, producers and marketeers of this piss have profited immensely from the bogan's love of convenience and fully integrated branding. The very words 'Ready-to-drink (RTD)' make its heart palpitate furiously, like a hipster about to watch a cardigan-clad Zooey Deschanel perform a duet with Tom Waits in front of a small organic farmers' market.

Knowing the bogan's helpless malleability in the face of televisual stimuli, it comes as no surprise that premixed drinks are one of the most heavily advertised alcoholic products in the country. Combining a vertigo-inducing array of cross-promotional advertising between various paragons of boganic activity at sick clubs, the premixed drink is literally the alcoholic equivalent of a Lynx can.

Allegedly premium Swedish vodka brand Absolut has, in true bogan-baiting form, taken their communication strategy to the maxtreme. In a display of absolut genius, in 2005 they introduced a slender, translucent bottle of Absolut vodka and a citrus mixer, and branded it 'Cut'. They employed the services of Maxxium Australia to distribute their swill and had the lovely folk at Naked Communications handle their advertising. This convergence of maximum nudity rocked the bogan's tectonic plates, causing an eruption of bogan dollars of Eyjafjallajökull-ian proportions. It could now be seen drinking Absolut Cut Lemon in Cut-branded bars, wearing the free promotional Cut rubber wristband and talking about how it would like to cut up the c*** that rubbed up against its missus.

Such is the bogan's love for the RTD that not even the application of a 70% tax served to meaningfully impede its predilection for ripping bulk piss in this form. Ignoring the fact that a 330 ml bottle of watermelon flavoured Bacardi Breezer now costs about the same as 330 ml of straight Bacardi rum, it will gravitate towards the pretty red coloured bottle like tinea to unwashed feet. The bogan is always ready to drink, and it likes its liquor and sugarwater to be the exact same way.

While the bogan's behaviour may seem erratic and purposeless, rest assured that it is not. Aware of the horror of an evening without premixes and remixes, the bogan will not stray far from venues that provide heady amounts of both of these things. The introduction of premixed cocktails was the next logical step towards capturing a larger share of the bogan's nocturnal leisure dollar. Now, young femme-bogues can make gut-wrenching jokes about sucking off cowboys and innovative quips about having sex on a beach while brandishing a slippery nipple.

SPIRITUALITY

Buddhist iconography as home furnishings

No longer is the bogan confined to decorating its home with HSV wall clocks and novelty stubby holders featuring grammatically reprehensible, jingoistic humour about beer guts, ageing or alleged sexual prowess. The 21st century has seen the bogan home politicised by the upwardly mobile sentiments of the female bogan, who is now pursuing new goals in the bedroom, kitchen, bathroom and dining room. Unfortunately for the male bogan, these goals do not provide opportunities to validate the assertions printed on its carefully selected stubby holders.

They are the new goals of the suburban aspirational class so elegantly segmented as Howard's battlers, and what better way to announce one's entry into the knowledge economy than by purchasing a Buddhism-themed figurine, statue or water feature from the garden section of Kmart. The female bogan is then able to experience an increased sense of affiliation with thousands of years of learning, sacrifice and suffering, conveniently distilled into a domestic decoration that will go well with the new cushions in the Grand Sitting Area. Fortunately for the household, the female does not expect the rest of the family to understand the philosophy behind the iconography, largely because she doesn't either.

Much like the destruction of polar bear habitat being wrought by the seemingly unstoppable march of global warming, the female bogan's bold new foray into exotic symbolism has forced the traditional male to retreat to the rumpus room. There, it is constructing a final battle line near the entrance to the room, comprised primarily of the stubby holders, and a scale model of a Bathurst-winning Holden driven by the late, great Peter Brock. To further ensure its 'manclave' is not encroached upon by the female, it will decorate the walls with posters of bikini-clad centrefolds from *Zoo Weekly*, stock the bar fridge with a fresh slab of Slates and purchase a home gym that it will not use.

Pandora bracelets

In Greek mythology, Pandora was the first woman, whom each god helped create by giving a unique gift. Unaware of this, millennia later, the female bogan strives to match her uniqueness, constantly on the hunt for new ways to express her individuality, though of course she could never do anything that would make her stand out *too* much from the crowd . . .

Enter Pandora. Launched in Denmark in 1982 by some clever Danish guy, the Pandora brand of jewellery appeals to the female bogan's love of shiny things, addictive consumption habits and ongoing quest for homogenous distinctiveness. For the uninitiated, Pandora sells relatively simple, affordable bracelets which are fitted with 'charms', little hoopy things coming in various shapes, sizes and materials.

The Pandora bracelet is perfect for the modern female bogan. The gold bracelet ($1700) is too expensive, so a silver one ($90) is selected. Everyone has one, but they're all 'totally unique' and representative of the bogan's deepest inner desires. Like getting another lamewad charm. A non-bogan understands subtlety and restraint, but the female bogan will always take things to the xtreme. She purchases charm after charm for her bracelet, adding a new one any time her credit card is accepted.

A silver heart to show her passion, star sign because of her love of horoscopes, a flower, a lucky horseshoe, a little froggy, a crucifix, a Buddha, an owl, a letter M for Mylyssa, an angel, a baby pram, a teddy, a special gold heart, a high-heeled shoe, a 'best friends', another flower, another flower, another flower, a swirly thing, a puzzle piece, a peace sign, a car, and a round thing with a dangly ball. The femme-bogue's quest is aided by her friends, family and other half, with Pandora charms a convenient, affordable ($30+) and relatively thoughtless gift for her birthday or anniversary.

A year later, the female bogan pauses to view the purchased DNA that is no longer in fashion, blissfully oblivious to the fact that the tacky piece of jewellery dangling from her wrist cost approximately $1900 to assemble. But every bogan agrees that this is a small price to pay for being xtremely unique and glamorous.

Vampires

It's Angel's fault, really. The success of *Buffy the Vampire Slayer* in the 1990s naturally and inexorably led to that most bogan of TV abominations, the spin-off. Bogans like nothing more than copies of TV shows they already like, so creating a show featuring the character of greatest bogan appeal means a whole new show without having to write new characters or scripts. While Angel was undeniably a more boring character than everyone else on *Buffy*, the evil geniuses in TV land knew that with his vampire-with-a-soul shtick, they had struck bogan gold.

The female bogan was unable to resist. She desires nothing so much as xtreme romance. While she often tells her disapproving friends that despite the tribal tatts and glass-induced facial scarring, her man is 'a real sweetie underneath', the vampire is a representation of the fantasy that her muscle-bound neolith cannot live up to. While the dangers of regular bogan romance may be limited to domestic violence and STDs, vampire romance is linked to transmogrification, shimmering and abstinence.

Like Richard Wilkins, the modern vampire is an empty shell, a vessel into which the female bogan can pour her frustrated sense of romance and danger. Despite the fact that the vampire most likely wants to kill and disfigure her, she has decided that, thanks to Angel, the vampire is merely misunderstood. Having the requisite level of danger (possibly homicidal) coupled with being relatively safe (he is a fictional character), the femme-bogue can sit back in bed at night and dream of Edward Cullen not-quite ravishing her.

After seeing *Twilight* – on Richard Wilkins' recommendation – the bogan decides to read all of the books. These books feature two key characters: a female character with absolutely no personality beyond whining about how awful her life is, and a vampire who is beautiful, kind, listens to the whining and glows in the dark . . . or something. And refuses to root her.

Despite the female bogan's embrace of hyper-sexualising herself and her children, she finds irresistibly arousing a book written by an abstinence-promoting Mormon about a 600-year-old teenaged vampire not wanting to 'bite' his nubile belle. In fact, the femme-bogue becomes so engorged by the notion of abstinence that she is likely to proceed post-haste to the local glassing barn to gyrate wildly against anyone not smelling strongly of garlic. This demonstrates the dizzying power that sexual innuendo and metaphor have over the bogan's copulatory glands.

Unfortunately, the bogan's inability to actually understand metaphor resulted in *True Blood*. Take vampires, give them a conscience, and have them engage in xtreme sex scenes with

Anna Paquin. The bogan, after all, doesn't understand abstinence either. Of any kind.

Ill-informed analysis of the Qur'an

The bogan holds a variety of convictions, which, while internally inconsistent, are rarely open to negotiation. These opinions are based largely on the incomprehensible and contradictory whisperings of the trashmedia Kraken. Because the bogan is just a soggy rodent in the waters of political discourse, it will cling to these convictions like a piece of barnacled flotsam in a particularly savage maelstrom. The bogan can often be seen shouting in an incoherent and grammatically incorrect fashion as it circles the political suckhole.

The bogan, uninterested in the high falutin' opinions of ivory tower academics, will not have studied the relevant subject matter in even the most cursory manner. Being from the 'real world', the bogan understands things on a higher level than a mere academic. It is just as well the bogan has a preternatural sense for how things are in the 'real world', because it gets its news and views as part of the blinkered programming of one of three commercial television networks.

When it comes to Islam, the bogan is particularly at sea. When its ginormous TV spits out brief, vague and highly coded news of events occurring in the Middle East, the bogan grips tighter to its barnacled flotsam. This particular flotsam comes in the form of the Qur'an, which the bogan knows on an intuitive level, without having read any of it or found out what happens in it.

The bogan will tell people that the Qur'an binds all Muslims to a thing called 'Shania's Law', which compels them to spread chaos and oppression throughout the globe. In the bogan's mind, Muslims of all stripes, each one a potential suicide bomber, have been fighting each other since before the time of Santa. This, the bogan believes, has all been in order to attain maxtreme quantities of virgins in the afterlife. The bogan is highly suspicious of this, as the bogan wants its virgins right away, without having to work for them.

In recent times, the bogan has become increasingly concerned that the thrice-locked boganic wonderland of Australia is under threat from these Shania's Law-following, virgin-motivated warriors. After all, Muslim terrorists were responsible for shutting down one of the best bars in Bali, and the bogan barely saved Cronulla from being the beachhead for an Islamic caliphate. But strangely, the threat of bombing has taken a back seat lately to the threat of garment-based attack. The bogan is continually haunted by the image of a women wearing the burqa, because the bogan prefers its women to be largely clothes-free, or at least to show a bit of exposed 'G'. Because the burqa deprives bogans of their fundamental right to leer at every woman equally, the bogan does not like the burqa. But when it tries to convince someone of this, the bogan may even give an uncharacteristic nod to the female liberation movement, before skipping infuriatingly to a carefully crafted theory detailing how Sheikh Alcopop is using Saudi oil dollars to launch a jihad on massive cans.

Baptisms

The bogan only recently learned what a hedge fund is. Even though, throughout the global financial turmoil of 2008 and 2009, it only heard snippets in the trashmedia about hedge funds collapsing, it feels now that it knows what they are. They are betting syndicates set up to bet on different things from what the bank bets on so that, no matter what, they always win. Whether or not this is true, the bogan has yet to realise that it has been engaging in its own hedge fund for some time. With its consonant-challenged progeny's eternal souls, no less.

Baptising their newborn, vowel-free spawn is the perfect way for the bogan, who is entirely indifferent to observant religion (it will not get up early on Sunday) to make sure that, just in case they're wrong, and the god they don't follow is a vengeful one, their kid is safe.

By baptising their child, the bogan counteracts all of the heinous acts it will no doubt commit throughout its life. It is a religious prepaid carbon offset for all of the filthy emissions that the bogan's child is likely to be encouraged or allowed to make by its lack of parenting. Little Aron's unfortunate dose of ADHD will, of course, provide a relatively ample amount of coverage from divine retribution, but it can't mask everything.

Moreover, baptisms are similar to weddings in that the bogan parents get to be the centre of attention for the day. The child, being of an unintelligible age and brain capacity, merely sits in the middle of any given room, while the profoundly fertile mum and dad sit beatifically nearby, wallowing in the cooing fervour that is a new child.

The bogan is also very aspirational. While this tends to focus on the corporeal realm, with its attendant McMansions and 86-inch 3D! televisions, the bogan will always aspire to bigger things. And to the bogan, eternal soft white light, feathered beds and no real concern with adultery (as the male bogan considers the place) is worth a quick dunk in the holy water and a deathbed repentance.

The bogan may invoke the name of god in a self-righteous fashion in order to bolster its arguments about everything from kids' fashion to foreign policy, but when road-raging, fighting, complaining about refugees or purchasing garish 'fashion' items, god couldn't be further from the bogan's mind. This doesn't stop the bogan from getting a priest to dunk its offspring in magical godwater, which is similar to nutrient water, but replaces theoretical nutritional content with theoretical spiritual content.

SPORTING LIFE

Tennis

This title is perhaps misleading. The bogan does not, in fact, enjoy tennis. Indeed, the bogan is utterly indifferent to tennis for 50 weeks of the year. But for those shining fourteen days in January, bogans empty their pockets into the coffers of tennis administrators when the Australian Open rolls into town.

Violently ignoring its aristocratic beginnings in the late 19th century, the bogan has ruined yet another event. Champagne and strawberries and cream have been replaced by Heineken and potato wedges, while grace and harmony have been forfeited as weak and unnecessary.

The bogan's sporadic racism is allowed to enter full bloom during these two weeks, as it selectively filters the global gathering of athletes in order to validate every one of its opinions about places it has never visited. This is best demonstrated by the attendance of bogans at any match containing an Australian. Or someone who was once married to an Australian.

Commentators, fostering this sense of 'patriotism', surreptitiously (and by surreptitiously, we mean blatantly and offensively) lend their support to players during their call of the game by referring to local players by their first names, and spending a great deal of time discussing their excellent play, while dismissing failures as a bit of luck on the part of their opponent. The TV coverage is even better for bogans in recent years as it contains less and less actual tennis, which is substituted for ongoing montages of close-ups of hot chicks hitting shots and grunting to remixed music. Following that will be the 'Hot Shots' segment, which distills an entire day's tennis down to four points which conclude with commentators saying 'whoa!'

This has hit a progressively larger snag year upon year, as Australian players have sucked more and more. The presence of overtly bogan players among the Australian elite has done little to slow the decline of interest in Australian players. As such, the commentators' attentions had to be lavished on others: to wit, top ten players and attractive female players. The bogan male can therefore spend a great deal of time watching women's sport – something it never, ever does – perving up ladies' dresses and skirts under the pretence of enjoying the action. Concurrently, the female bogan can spend a great deal of time watching women's sport – something it never, ever does – checking out 'fashion' under the pretence of enjoying the action.

Having enjoyed the illicit thrill of looking at women's underwear for some time, the bogan male will then pick up the *Herald Sun*, *Daily Telegraph* or related non-*Australian* News Corp paper and glance fleetingly at the headline. This will prompt a long-winded denunciation of the 'Croatian fuckwits' behaving like bogans while wearing the wrong flag as a cape and ruining the tennis by getting into fights. Politicians and social commentators then reinforce the belief that foreigners should be banned from watching such a quintessentially Australian sport. The bogan then looks at its watch, realises it's late for the 20/20 game and leaves. It then returns, sheepishly, one hour later, explaining to all who'll listen that the security guards at the cricket are all fuckwits.

Twenty/twenty cricket

The bowler turns on his heel as he approaches the top of his run, tosses the ball from hand to hand, steam very nearly bursting out of his nostrils given the furious energy he has built up leading into this moment. Gradually, he begins his run, first at an amble, then a run, before hitting the crease at an Olympian sprint, simultaneously throwing his arm over his shoulder and releasing his small leather projectile at his nemesis at nigh-on 100 miles an hour. The die is cast, the first delivery bowled in anger of what will hopefully be an epic contest.

The batsman, in a split second, sizes up the speed, trajectory, movement and bounce of the ball. Instantly, he assesses the placings of the fielders, the chances of success. He's facing a great bowler with a head full of steam, and he's yet to find his rhythm. He steps forward, raises his left elbow, presents a straight bat, and sends the ball safely back to the other end of the pitch. Game on.

Then, from the crowd, emerges: 'Fucking hit the thing, you lazy c***! It's twenty/twenty!'

Welcome to twenty/twenty (or in the bogan-abbreviated, text-speak vernacular, T20) cricket. Cricket, 30 years ago, was abridged for the nascent bogan into World Series Cricket – taking the traditional five-day, 450-over epics and trimming them down to a neat 100 so that they could all be bowled in time for bed. Colourful clothes and night games were the norm, and bogans embraced the maxtreme spectacle of cricket for the attention-deficient.

However, as is always the bogan way, turning a five-day sporting event into an eight-hour sporting event was not enough. Thus, from the depths of the mother country, T20 was born. Cutting back like a newspaper editor who just saw his daughter reading *TMZ*, cricket was whittled away to a positively skeletal 40 overs, creating the ability to finish a match in three hours.

Of course, xtreme brevity was not sufficient to mollify the bogans' impatience for sixes and fours. Cricket geniuses incorporated 'power plays' from one-day cricket, because clearly the bogan enjoys power of any sort, its total lack of awareness of what power plays are or their effect notwithstanding.

The boundaries were moved even closer to the batsmen, almost guaranteeing that if they closed their eyes and connected, said fours and sixes would ensue. And naturally, when these inevitable fours and sixes are scored, the bogan masses, clad as they are in flag-capes and cheap knock-offs of the Australian uniform, can celebrate. Celebrate along with fireworks. Fireworks that are effectively large stoves, spewing forth flame, allowing one household's annual natural gas consumption to be spent igniting flame bursts on the sidelines. Meanwhile, over the loudspeakers, 'Who Let the Dogs Out' pumps, elevating the bogan to a new level of patriotic hysteria. Meanwhile, at the pub among those already kicked out, a bogan glasses someone.

Mixed martial arts

Boasting a decade of experience in watching reality TV, the bogan knows what's real. This knowledge of reality initially proved to be burdensome as, after 20 years of watching WWF/WWE 'pro wrestling', it caused a looming suspicion to form at the back of the bogan's mind regarding the authenticity of what it once thought was the apex of all things xtreme. Then, like a whisper on the wind, it began to hear rumours. It heard that, somewhere, there was a cage that was not in the back of a divvy van. This cage had fighters. These fighters were xtreme. So xtreme that intellectuals were trying to ban them. It was bogan crack.

Eventually, it emerged that it was a new sport called 'Ultimate

Fighting'. The bogan dissolved under the weight of its own surging endorphins. Upon closer inspection, the bogan realised just how amazing this new sport was. It answered the question that has been preoccupying the bogan since *Bloodsport* was released. Who would win if a kung fu dude and a karate dude got into a massive, glass-free stoush?

Initially branded under the slogan 'There Are No Rules', the 'Ultimate Fighting Championship' (UFC) promoters found themselves straining under the weight of a bogan tsunami, as the bogan has lived its life espousing the idea that it was no follower of mere rules. Then, the bogan discovered something shocking. After a period of political backlash, new rules were introduced to prevent death. This was, to the bogan, unacceptable. It was no longer ultimate enough. But only for a moment. In a flash of inspiration, the bogan realised that there were now at least 31 different ways to break the rules. To top it off, the sport began branding itself as 'mixed martial arts' (MMA) to the masses, while remaining 'Ultimate Fighting' to the bogans. The bogan didn't stand a chance.

The bogan then learned of Randy 'The Natural' Couture, a fighter in America's UFC. The bogan no longer just wanted its clothes couture, but its violence as well. Then, in 2005, a reality TV show called *The Ultimate Fighter*, which followed *WWE Raw* on pay TV, brought UFC to the bogan world in the most awesomely appropriate way possible. It taught the bogan that UFC is the ultimate in xtreme – it has cages. It has blood. It has dudes who spend a great deal of time getting huge. The bogan then learned of dedicated MMA training programs – a veritable primordial soup of huge bogans who were tired of having to resort to glassware as a weapon, and who considered regular martial arts to be not nearly xtreme enough – held in Phuket. Perfect.

But none of this was what won the bogan over. They had the bogan at 'Ultimate Fighting'.

Buying a snowboard

Each winter, the bogan stares balefully out of its window, through the sleeting rain, and dreams of being maxtreme. The sun has gone, and the bogan can no longer visit the beach once a month, wander around shirtless and pretend to know how to surf. Its fantasies of warm-weather maxtremity dashed for four months, it has been reduced to a blithering mess of sporting brand-free misery.

Then, sometime around mid-June, the bogan is watching breakfast TV. Glumly shovelling Nutri-Grain into its mouth, it notices something different. After the obligatory dwarf weather segment, the robot host cuts to a new character, one the bogan vaguely remembers, swathed in brightly coloured Michelin tyres, and its muffled voice speaks into a microphone about 'crisp powder', 'lifts operating' and 'black runs'. Setting aside its iron man food, the bogan pays attention to this human marshmallow. And it comes to a realisation; it has found winter nirvana. Australia has snow. And snow people are exactly like beach people, but with snow. The bogan immediately buys a snowboard. And not just any snowboard . . . a snowboard that can achieve maximum altitude. A snowboard that will get it up to X-Games standards. After all, if that 16-year-old kid at the Winter Olympics can do it with a broken hand, surely the bogan can do it with its broken grip on reality?

Upon arrival at the lodge, the bogan will automatically adopt the local vernacular in spectacularly unconvincing fashion. It will speak of 'hitting the slopes', 'carving it up' and refer tangentially to 'whistler' as a snowboarding manoeuvre. It will troll around the lodge keeping one eye peeled, as it has always dreamed of hunting the extremely rare, highly seasonal, arctic cougar. It will be happy, as this entire exercise has offered it an opportunity to acquire an array of garish, brightly coloured, heavily branded specialty clothing, without actually having to go outside and get cold and/or wet.

Emerging groggily onto the slopes the next morning, the bogan decides it should give its shiny new equipment a practice run. Naturally, upon hearing that 'black run' means the most maxtreme, the bogan decides to enact its newly remixed winter dreams on the crisp powder. Lessons are for pussies without natural talent. Thirty minutes in, the bogan decides that the inability to snowboard is actually called 'freestyle', and henceforth tells it to anyone who will listen.

Come summer, the bogan will look gaily out of its window at the bright sunshine, and glance fleetingly, scornfully, at the hot-pink snowboard in the corner, before heading out and buying a surfboard. And not just any surfboard . . .

Home fitness equipment

The bogan wants a rockin' body. It wants to trim down the fat, tone up and, in the case of the male, get ripped, vascular and generally huge. It wants to finally get the respect it deserves. It wants to be noticed by the opposite sex. To be more confident. More successful. More energetic. But getting a sweet rig is hard. A true Aussie battler, the bogan works roughly eight hours per day, five days per week, and therefore simply does not have time in its 128 remaining weekly hours to get to the gym. Going for a run is also out of the question, as this would require venturing outdoors beyond the minimum distance required to get from building to vehicle, or vice versa.

If only there were some kind of quick, easy way for the bogan to achieve the body it has always dreamed of without leaving the comfort of its own home, or missing *Australia's Got Talent*. Watching Kerri-Anne during a hangover-induced sickie one morning, it discovers the shortcut it has been searching for. The Ab Krusher, as demonstrated by a pair of orange skinned, all-American models. The quarterback and the cheerleader. The male ripped, jacked, vascular. The female lean, toned, svelte. Both sporting hazardous amounts of silicone and teeth whitener. All that is required of the bogan in order to attain an equivalent level of synthetic perfection is six easy payments of $69.95.

Upon arrival of its shiny new Ab Demolisher, the bogan parks itself in front of the plasma, ready to start shedding kilos. Three minutes in, it knows something is wrong. It is not beaming a radioactive smile. Its pecs are not glistening. No muscle tone has yet become visible. This is nothing like the infomercial. Following a few subsequent sporadic attempts, the Ab Slayer is deposited in the garage, never to be seen again, with the bogan claiming the apparatus caused it to do its back in.

At the turn of the new year, the bogan once again resolves to get fit, this time purchasing the Ab King ProMax. The inevitable cycle repeats like clockwork with the passing of each year, as the bogan chews through the Ab Cruncher, Ab Rocker, Ab Roller, Ab Revolutioniser, Ab Terminator, and Ab Abu Ghraib. Finally, the bogan concludes that its inability to achieve physical fitness is related to a glandular condition, allergies and/or ADHD.

WHEELS

Personalised numberplates

All people seek to express their personality through their actions, possessions and personal presentation. Because the bogan has more personality than the rest of us, it requires more canvases upon which to portray its traits. One of these canvases is the lower back, but another important one is the numberplate of the bogan's car. While all cars come with numberplates, for the bogan that rectangular piece of metal is more than a registration tool – it is an existential statement of identity and intent.

State traffic authorities have identified this need in the bogan and offer a suite of solutions. For a price of hundreds of dollars (and an additional annual fee of hundreds of dollars), the bogan is able to use the front and rear of its vehicle to announce its multicoloured manifesto to the world, provided it is six characters or less. Undeterred, inventive alphanumeric abbreviations are employed, the skills for which have been honed through years of virtually illegible text messaging. The message of the numberplate usually refers to the car's ability to attain speed, or the alleged importance or desirability of its owner. Examples include 'WTABUZ', '2HOT4U', and 'COPB8'. On other occasions the numberplate is a variant of the driver's name, though the motivation behind such a choice is unclear, since the bogan doesn't spend its time outside of the car with a name tag pinned to its shirt. Often, the bogan will seek to remove the badging from the rear bumper of the car to make it seem more subtle, yet describe the make or model of the car on the numberplate in far larger letters.

The personalisation of the numberplate is believed to make it easier for the bogan to locate its vehicle in shopping centre carparks, as well as intimidating or impressing other bogans during Friday night repetitive laps up and down a street that has fashionable shops on it. By having a personalised numberplate, the male bogan can prove to prospective mating partners that the car is not stolen or his parents', underlining his suitability as a father and provider to her children.

Petrol consumption as recreation

Perhaps the bogan's obsession with attaining toys as a grown adult can be explained as an effort to address the lingering trauma of having been denied them as a child, or, conversely, as a direct result of having been given everything it cried, kicked and bit hard enough for. What's certain is that when it developed from its larval state to its full-grown adult form, the bogan's appetite for toys only got stronger and more reliant on the depletion of our planet's petroleum resources.

Much like his anthropological forebears, one of the defining experiences for the nouveau bogan is being at the controls of a vehicle over 100 times more powerful than function strictly requires. But in comparison to the proto-bogan, satisfied with merely speeding his Falcon GT and possibly lighting 'em up within earshot of some bogan skirt, one of the modern bogan's greatest achievements has been hugely expanding the options for satisfying his impulse to consume genocidal quantities of fossil fuels. Power boats, dirt bikes, four wheelers, go-karts, dune buggies, generators, asphalters, bobcats, bonfires – the rule is, if you can put petrol in it, the new bogan loves it, will get it on credit and disregard all operational manuals in effecting its prompt destruction.

While his father may have gotten his bogan on by leaving a beach strewn with empty tinnies and Winfield butts, and pissing in clear sight of nearby families, today's bogan takes beach-based obnoxiousness to new levels with the introduction of the jet ski. Not only can today's bogan show off his appalling trailer-reversing technique (extra bogan points if a petrol-powered device comes with its own trailer) but upon firing it up, he can shower those nearby with oil-smeared water and black smoke and, crucially, emit a noise so obscenely loud it aurally bludgeons the entire coastline into a hasty retreat. Thus he achieves the holy trinity of bogan – air pollution, water pollution and sound pollution. In this heightened state, our subject utilises the rest of the afternoon exhibiting his proficiency for bogans' enduring contribution to motorsport – the doughnut – upon the novel canvas of water.

'Holdens'

Not to be confused with the Chav, the bogan's British cousin, the new bogan male now wants to be a Chev. This utterly confusing phenomenon involves removing the Holden badging from a Monaro or SS Commodore and replacing it with a badge from a bankrupt American company. While the bogan will sometimes profess a desire to visit the vacuous crassness that is Las Vegas, it has generally been unfashionable during the last decade for the nouveau bogue to be overtly pro-American. Except on his Australian car.

The entire Holden Commodore range is designed and built in Australia. The Australian operation designs and builds an engine that is exported to numerous other countries in which its parent company operates. In the same manner, some Holden cars in Australia use a V8 engine originally designed overseas by General Motors, and also used in Hummer, Buick, Chevrolet, Saab,

Vauxhaul, Pontiac, Cadillac and GMC vehicles. The bogan has a fundamental craving to be seen as tough, and somewhere along the line he incorrectly decides that the V8 engine in his car is a Chevrolet. Making the entire vehicle, by rational extension, actually a Chevrolet. The bogan is seemingly ashamed to drive Australian. This logic flaw is not applied to the VL Commodore from the late eighties, which used a Nissan engine. Because Japanese people aren't tough, and the bogan needs to be tough.

The term 'the Stranger' was coined for the process of sitting on one's hand until it goes numb, and then browsing pornography. The lack of sensation in the hand simulates the experience of receiving manual assistance from someone else. In the same way, the bogan will drink locally brewed, foreign label beer until its brain goes numb. It will then disregard its otherwise rampant Australian nationalism, enthusiastically ripping the Holden badges off its car and replacing them with a set of Chevy logos. With its car suitably enhanced, the bogan endlessly prowls the roads of nightclub districts, attempting to trick similarly uninformed bogan females into believing that he is an exotic lothario, a rare and irresistible sexual force from across the seas. All too often, the evening ends with the bogan covertly performing the Stranger on itself in a nearby carpark.

Road rage

While the bogan generally engages in few critically time-important activities and has accrued a lifetime of missed deadlines, when on the road it is in an urgent hurry. If delayed by a stop sign, it will charge through. If delayed by a line of traffic, it will seek to drive in the emergency lane. It will reach its destination a full 90 seconds earlier than the non-bogan, and it will consume that 90 seconds, along with 300 other seconds, to stake out a parking space that is 30 steps closer to Boost Juice.

However, the bogan's notoriously poor coping skills make it susceptible to losing its cool entirely if it finds that the traffic conditions are not to its liking. A key problem of road-based bogans is that a car makes a bogan invincible. Encased in a 1500-kilogram glass and steel shell, the bogan transmogrifies from a dull irritation into a dangerous menace. It enforces its skewed value system and desire for the maxtreme by speeding, running red lights and burning rubber, disregarding other road rules as it sees fit. If someone does not let the bogan do these things as it wishes, the bogan wants justice, and that's where the real trouble starts.

Just as it will do in relation to free speech, the bogan sees itself as entitled to break any road rule. This entitlement is extended to exactly zero per cent of other road users, including other road users driving safely and correctly. If someone merges into a lane in front of a bogan, the results will depend on a number of factors:

- How badly it wants to go to the shopping centre or nightclub strip.
- Whether the bogan is intoxicated.
- The presence of tribal tattoos.
- Any other obstacles that the bogan has encountered that day.
- The presence of personalised numberplates.
- Degree to which the offending motorist is perceived to be Asian.

If the bogan's anger becomes moderate, it will scream from inside its car, and make obscene gestures. It is unlikely to realise that the other person cannot hear its profanities from inside their own car, but this does not deter it from pursuing this action with vigour. If the anger level becomes high, the bogan will attempt to overtake the other car without indicating, expecting surrounding cars to part like Katie Price's legs. If it is not allowed to re-enter its original lane, it will emerge from its car in a blind fury. The alpha road warrior bogan will attempt to lure the other driver from their car with an elaborate roadside war dance, intermittently spitting and kicking door panels. If this is not successful, it will eventually return to its car, do a burnout, and rocket off into the distance, which is usually the next traffic light 100 metres up the road.

Party buses

The bogan does not like public transport. It will, whenever possible, burn the maximum amount of fossil fuels it can in order to get from A to B, occasionally via L. While it has, over the course of the past five or so years, migrated swiftly into newly gentrified inner suburbs, the bogan has brought with it its deeply held love of driving any distance more than 200 metres away. As such, despite now living less than five minutes' walk from almost every necessary service, the bogan will drive three minutes to the gym to walk on a treadmill for half an hour or lift weights of Warner Brothers-esque proportions. The bogan won't be seen dead on a train, unless it's the first train on a Sunday morning, which it can then advertise to its cohorts in an effort to demonstrate its capacity for maxtreme partying. Trams are for latte-sipping poofs. Buses are barely mentioned. But there is one bus, aside from the Vengabus, that no bogan can resist the lure of: the party bus.

A mobile bogan convention of epic proportions, the party bus (or in the original Latin, *buseus boganicus*) has become the vehicle of choice of partying bogans with short attention spans who cannot afford a stretch Hummer or else know too many other bogans to fit in one. The party bus will take the bogans to many, many bogan venues over the course of four hours, charging the bogan great amounts of money for what is in effect a large, smelly taxi. Irregardless, the bogan bus is now home to every conceivable bogan celebration, of which three feature predominantly: 21st birthdays, buck's nights and, especially, hens' nights. During these sessions, the boguettes will engage in a variety of thrilling activities, from truth or dare games to fake orgasm and pole dancing competitions, to all guided by their trusty host, Steve.

No one knows where these hosts go during the day, but they appear to be some kind of supra-bogan. It is as if they were once bogans but have transcended into a state of pure boganic energy, emerging in corporeal form only to guide confused and disoriented bogans around the CBD to ever more seedy bars before popping last year's designer drug and trying to nail the hen's best friend/ drunkest chick there.

If you encounter a bogan bus in the wild, the wisest course of action is not to turn around, not to run: resist the natural human inclination to flee and simply back away slowly until you are at a safe distance; at which point you should calmly turn around and take to your heels. Once you've gone, the participants in the maxtreme bogan party session will search for some missing companion named Rachael, who was last seen at Velour Bar with trusty Steve, before heading off and leaving her to catch the first train home tomorrow morning.

Epil●gue:

Being proud

Despite never having achieved anything of note, the bogan is a proud creature. Paradoxically, finding pride in a bottomless pit of mediocrity is in itself, perhaps, by some strand of backward bogan logic, something to be proud of. For the bogan is an underdog, a dark horse, an Aussie battler. It has toiled endlessly against the cruel injustices faced throughout its comfortable, cosseted life. The ADHD. The allergies. Political correctness gone mad. The enormous monthly interest bill on its McMansion, investment property and line of personal credit. A complete lack of patience, discipline and forethought.

The bogan has overcome all of these unavoidable hardships to find pride in some great achievements. Like being born in Australia, and the time 'we' stuck it to the Poms in the Ashes, or to the Turks at Gallipoli. Like the kid from their school who went on to be a professional football player. Like the fact that the bogan's city is better than any other city. The bogan is proud, too, of all the people it went to school with who went on to succeed at things the bogan knows it could also have succeeded at, if it chose to. And the bogan is proud of various other achievements that it did not contribute to and had barely a tangential connection with, but still describes with phrases such as 'we smashed 'em'.

The bogan is proud that it helped Delta Goodrem recover from cancer, proud of its oversized, heavily branded Louis Vuitton bag, proud that it got back to its pre-baby weight, even if it meant ignoring basic nutrition, proud that it accepts foreigners because it listens to 'Paper Planes', even if it can't pronounce her real name. Having never made it beyond the 'my dad is tougher than your dad' stage of mental development, the bogan remains able to project the successes and desirable characteristics of others onto itself. In a convenient twist of evolution, however, the bogan has managed to retain the ability to blame others for all of its own personal failures.

The bogan, proud of itself, its enormous cans, enormous guns and enormous sense of self-worth, is well prepared for life. It sits down in front of the television to watch Aussie Russell Crowe in *Gladiator*, while listening to that awesome Aussie band, Crowded House, and eating that fantastic Aussie food, Vegemite. The bogan is happy in its adopted cocoon of pride.

Maxtreme Updated Epilogue

Since this book was first released the bogan has further cemented its place in modern society This is as it should be as the bogan understands the universe. From the big bang that started everything approximately 13.75 billion years ago, to *The Big Bang Theory* that started on Channel 9 on March 12, 2008, the bogan soars over space and time, like a golden, winged jet ski with the ability to transcend all of existence.

Contemplating its own constitutional right to eternity, the bogan intermittently sought refuge in the afterlife offered at its local megachurch. Returning to its McMansion, it would then ponder Buddhist reincarnation while focusing its eyes on the various pieces of Buddhist iconography that it had commandeered as domestic decoration. As the complexity of rebirth and multiple lives began to reveal itself to the bogan, it realised that it would need at least four of its child's Ritalin tablets to complete this train of thought.

The bogan, it did not sleep that night. Pacing between its rumpus room, its family room, its lounge room, its formal living room, its theatre, its dining room, and its informal eating area, concepts flew like lonely comets in the vast expanses of inky black sky. Karma, immortality, birth, death, lifespans, heaven, purgatory, rebirth. The first light of dawn brought no more relief than the three massive cans it had gasped down since 4am. It would need to drive its car. Driving its car would bring freedom. The ability to speed away from its troubles.

But going 80km/h didn't work. Paralysing thoughts of universe still present. 100km/h. A slight improvement in wellbeing. But the bogan did not aspire to a slight improvement in its wellbeing. It wanted maxtreme wellness. To be so well that it shat multi-vitamins. At that moment rays of sunlight scrambled over the Bunnings Warehouse on the horizon, and everything was illuminated in the bogan's mind. All of these big ideas about reincarnation and eternal life could be completely scrapped. **Y**ou **O**nly **L**ive **O**nce.

'F*%%^##ken YOLO!!!', the newly liberated bogan whooped, plunging its foot onto the accelerator pedal. The subsequent 8 minutes between this moment and the flashing lights of the police car were pure existential bliss.

YOLO neatly distils boganity into a blunt, four letter weapon that the bogan can use to attack anything that has a passing resemblance to a good idea, and embrace anything that is profoundly idiotic. Angry Angus burger with 56.5 grams of fat? YOLO. Interest-free finance with an interest rate of 20%? YOLO. Saving a portion of its salary each month? Nah, YOLO. 150km/h therapeutic morning spin through the suburbs? YOLO. Back alley

Thailand tetanus tattoo of YOLO in gothic font? Well . . . YOLO. The bogan only lives once, and is determined to make that once as brief as possible.

Temporarily deflated by its run-in with the local constabulary, the bogan rolled back to its McMansion at 5km/h below the speed limit. Still jittery from the heady mix of Ritalin, caffeine, guarana, adrenaline, and a $400 fine, it resolved to pull a sickie and soothe itself by watching the hilarious adventures of Leonard, Sheldon, and the whole *Big Bang Theory* gang on its Blu-Ray 3D LED LCD HD HDMI USB 100HZ TV. There would be no more troublesome thinking that day.

****

Since the publication of *Things Bogans Like*, E. Chas McSween et al (minus one) have often met for a beer with no English on the label. For them the burden of research into the bogan is ongoing. The publication of *Boganomics* gave them scope to broaden their published work (score a grant or two) and helped record the impact of the bogan and its interactions in all Australian life. But they too have learnt the truth of YOLO.

Tragically one contributor, Michael Jayfox, is no longer able to meet his colleagues in a laneway bar. His loss is felt by each of his fellow contributors, who still haven't come to terms with his death. After seeing *Boganomics* in print he felt he had only one other vision to pursue and so he chose to fulfil his dream and did indeed attempt to jump a shark while water-skiing and reciting Chaucer. Only a shredded wetsuit has been found. Thankfully, his research lives on and in his memory this updated, cheaper, more compact edition of *Things Bogans Like* includes Jayfox's famous research on the geographical distribution of the bogan. Use this guide to either avoid or mate with a bogan, whichever you find most appealing.

Domestic distribution of the bogan

Due to the enabling factor of both land and air transport, the bogan has colonised a broad geographic range of the Australian landmass. In Australia's tropics the warm weather enables the bogan to be shirtless, while in the southern reaches of the continent, the bogan is also shirtless, and attempting to convince others that it is impervious to the cold. Figure 1, below, details the parts of Australia where bogans have settled and where bogan sightings have been reported.

In addition to the land areas included in Figure 1, the invention of the jet ski by the Melbourne band Jet about fifteen years ago has enabled the bogan to confidently explore Australia's marine areas, either alone or in pairs. The rise of the jet ski imperilled dolphins and other aquatic life even more than the speedboat,

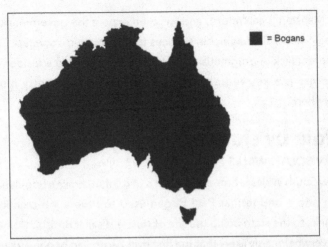

Figure 1 Geographical distribution of bogans in Australia

which was invented by Brisbane reggae trio REO Speedwagon in 1971.

Fond of the habitat of Australia's largest cities, the twenty-first century bogan is not confined to a particular suburb or side of town. While infamously fond of anywhere it is able to build a massive McMansion, the bogan can be found in the inner suburbs near trendy bars, in the suburbs miles from anywhere interesting or out of town trying to build a maxtreme dirt jump for its car. The broad geographic and financial range of the modern bogan means that whoever you are, and wherever you live, you may well be enduring one or more bogans next door.

The bogan has a different philosophy to the non-bogan when it comes to choosing a place to live. While the non-bogan will weigh up the local amenities and linkages of an area it wishes to reside in, the bogan will purchase whatever allows it to fit the largest

McMansion it can afford, and will then expect the government to magic-wand all imaginable services to the boganic doorstep. This inherent lack of pragmatism and logic when selecting a residential address is a key reason why bogans can end up pretty much anywhere.

State by state
NEW SOUTH WALES

New South Wales is home to almost a third of Australia's population and also a bridge that Paul Hogan used to have a job painting. Thanks to the state being the site of Australia's first British colony, it is overwhelmingly likely that the first ever Australian bogan arose in New South Wales. The time since then has seen the state develop immensely, which was validated by the fact that Russell Crowe (one of Australia's foremost adopted bogans) chose to settle in New South Wales when he left New Zealand as an adult.

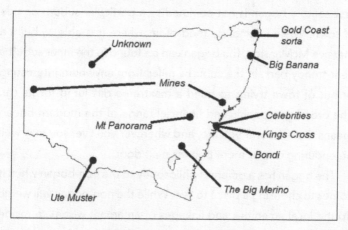

Figure 2 New South Wales

What's in it for the bogan?

The diversity of options available in New South Wales means that the bogan's short attention span need not be an obstacle to keeping occupied. Bogan-approved activities include vomiting in Kings Cross, trawling for Swedish backpackers at Bondi Beach, perspective-based photo opportunities at the Big Banana in Coffs Harbour, drinking at bars at Thredbo, and getting sunburnt on a part of the Gold Coast (albeit the boring bit).

VICTORIA

While Victoria is further from Bali and Phuket than any other mainland state, it is still a region that is prized by the bogan. In addition to the illustrious tales of Ned Kelly and Chopper Read, pretty much all of the stuff that happened during the first season of *Underbelly* happened in Victoria, so the bogan knows that Australia's south-east corner is capable of delivering maxtreme

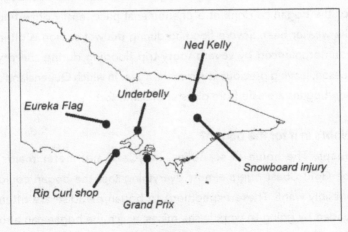

Figure 3 Victoria

bogan-friendly crime. Home to Australia's largest brewing company, Victorian liquor has also been responsible for millions of unplanned bogan pregnancies.

What's in it for the bogan?

Featuring two different grands prix, a massive casino that shoots balls of flame and a 100,000-seat shrine to Shane Warne and Brendan Fevola, the bogan is often willing to forgo its constitutional right to get sunburnt during winter in order to spend time in Victoria. If sunburn is still required, the bogan can head to Bells Beach during its summer holidays and fall off its surfboard.

QUEENSLAND

Australia's sunshine state has lured bogans for generations with the dual promises of Bundaberg Rum and cola on tap, and melanomas. Oh, and the Gold Coast. While the dominant local beer is only mid-strength in order to reduce glassings, the weather is warm enough for the bogan to drink at a phenomenal pace, easily offsetting the weaker beer. Severe flooding during the wet season is often counterbalanced by severe footy-trip flooding during the dry season, leaving precious few months a year in which Queensland's non-bogans are safe from disaster of some sort.

What's in it for the bogan?

Heaps. The home of schoolies, IndyCars, and meter maids, the Gold Coast offers almost everything that the bogan could possibly want. These expeditions to bogan paradise are often funded by going to work in the mines, which the bogan can also do in Queensland. A visiting bogan can acquire a Three-park

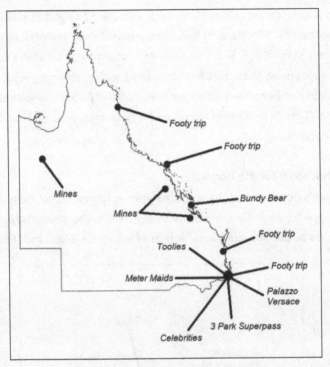

Figure 4 Queensland

Superpass, stay where the celebs stay at Palazzo Versace, check out the place where a stingray got the better of Steve Irwin or visit the Bundy factory to see where the magic happens.

SOUTH AUSTRALIA

As Australia's only state that wasn't founded as a convict settlement, it can be argued that boganism came later to South Australia than other areas. Despite this, the bogan has still managed to have a major impact. The South Australian bogan has endured significant setbacks in recent years, with the F1 Grand Prix being poached by Victoria, and hometown hero Lleyton Hewitt's tennis career stagnating. But – proudly for the bogan – Lleyton's lack of success on the court has coincided with a stunning level of success at becoming a bigger bogan. South Australia was also Julia Gillard's childhood home, and is presumably responsible for her accent.

What's in it for the bogan?

There's not too much here for the visiting bogan, aside from the chance to drink Coopers at its source. While the state currently serves as the second-favourite butt of interstate jokes, the future

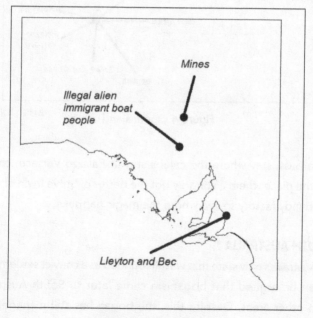

Figure 5 South Australia

expansion of BHP Billiton's massive Olympic Dam mining project promises to change the bogan's perception of South Australia. As a result, now is a good time to open a jet ski dealership and corner the market.

WESTERN AUSTRALIA

The Promised Land. Covering a third of Australia's landmass, Western Australia is universally considered by male bogans to be the solution to all of their self-inflicted problems. Going to

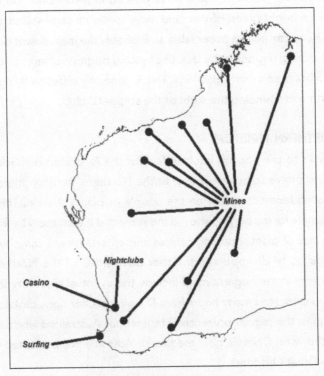

Figure 6 Western Australia

work in the mines can make even the least meritorious of bogans wealthy, allowing them to fly into Perth, lose at poker, smoke cigars and then glass someone in Northbridge at 2 a.m. At various points in its history Western Australia has had a secessionist movement, believed to have been driven by local bogans who don't want their eastern-seaboard brethren to be cashed up like them.

What's in it for the bogan?

Pretty much everything it's ever wanted. More coastline than you can poke a jet ski at, more underpoliced highway than you can poke a bright green HSV at, and more six-figure semi-skilled jobs than you can poke a poker table at. Probably the main downside to the mining regions is the dearth of young bogan women, causing squabbles and many glassings. This is generally offset by flying to Perth and spending the night at the strippers' club.

NORTHERN TERRITORY

Thanks to the bogan's intuitive feel for the Australian outback, it doesn't have to actually travel to the Northern Territory in order to confidently comment on the people or places therein. This is fortunate for the bogan, who – in the event that it visits the NT – finds the lack of giant shopping centres and entertainment complexes to be quite disappointing. Other downsides of the Northern Territory in the bogan's mind include the eventual discovery that Uluru is located many hours from Darwin and, for nonindigenous bogans, the regular presence of Indigenous Australians who have neither won Olympic gold medals for Australia nor presented on *The Great Outdoors*.

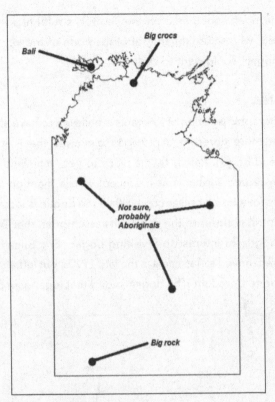

Figure 7 Northern Territory

What's in it for the bogan?

While the shopping centres aren't big enough, the crocodiles are. Numerous visiting bogans touring the Top End have endured severe injuries courtesy of crocodiles too stupid to understand that the bogan was 'just having a laugh'. Injuries aside, the crocodiles are quite big. Also big is Uluru, which the bogan can climb on or pose for perspective-based photographs in front of. In January

2007 the open speed limit on the Territory's rural highways was abolished, which consequently abolished one of the key reasons why a bogan would want to visit.

TASMANIA

The geographic isolation of Tasmania is believed to have allowed a different, more inbred strain of bogan to evolve – that is, if you ask a mainland bogan. Rather than a place to visit, mainland bogans primarily regard Tasmania as a concept whose mention can turn a terrible joke into a brilliant one. While the bogan is incorrect on this count, it is closer to the mark in its assumption that Tasmania contains little of interest to a visiting bogan. Eric Bana imitator Mark Read moved to Tasmania in the late 1990s, but left after a few years due to boredom. The bogan knows that legendary beer pit

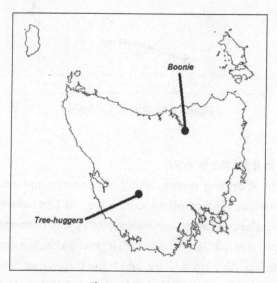

Figure 8 Tasmania

David Boon is down there somewhere – but he, like the thylacine, is rarely sighted.

What's in it for the bogan?

The bogan is aware that Tasmania produces good beer, but most of these products are sent to the mainland, thereby neutralising the incentive for the bogan to fly south to consume. The bogan's love of maxtremely big things does not extend to towering stands of eucalypt; in fact, the relative prominence of conservationists in Tasmania displeases the bogan. To conclude: while there are indeed bogans living in Tasmania, there is little reason for non-Tasmanian bogans to be sighted there.

AUSTRALIAN CAPITAL TERRITORY

The Australian Capital Territory covers an area of 2358 square kilometres and was carved out of New South Wales in 1911 to house a city that would go on to impose limits upon the bogan. Canberra is the demonic vacuum that removes the bogan's hardearned taxpayer dollars, for which the bogan vows it sees so little in return. In a bid to sweeten the deal and prevent bogans from laying waste to the city, the finest bogan bribes that the bogan has seen have originated from within the ACT, generally around election time. For the other 2.7 years out of three, the bogan knows that the entire Australian Capital Territory needs to be sacked.

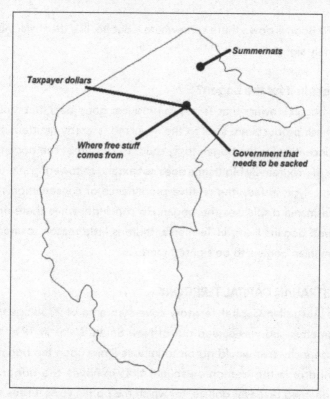

Figure 9 Australian Capital Territory

What's in it for the bogan?

A bogan visiting Canberra cannot expect to receive additional bogan bribes as a result of its journey, making a visit a reasonably pointless undertaking. On the plus side, the city is home to the time-/bogan-honoured institution called Summernats, where bogans can spend days on end watching other bogans do burnouts and then do some of their own. Parliament House is also host to the largest potential flag cape in the world.